Spells

The Ultimate Full-color Guide

Spells

Tabatha Jennings

Astrolog Publishing House Ltd.

Cover Design: Na'ama Yaffe
Language Consultants: Marion Duman, Carole Koplow
Layout and Graphics: Daniel Akerman
Production Manager: Dan Gold

P. O. Box 1123, Hod Hasharon 45111, Israel
Tel: 972-9-7412044
Fax: 972-9-7442714

© Astrolog Publishing House Ltd. 2003

ISBN 965-494-148-1

All rights reserved. No part of this publication may be reproduced, stored in a retrieval system, or transmitted, in any form or by any means, electronic, mechanical, photocopying, recording or otherwise, without the prior permission of the publisher.
Published by Astrolog Publishing House 2003

10 9 8 7 6 5 4 3 2 1

Contents

Introduction	7	To fulfill your desires	46
To bring back your lost love	8	Relief of pain (for someone else)	47
Attracting a mate	10	To create a stronger attraction	48
To find a love partner	12	To draw your lover's attention to you	49
To increase your attractiveness	14	Gambling or investment luck	50
To win someone's heart	15	To decide between two lovers	52
Attracting a romantic relationship	16	Attracting fast money for a specific purpose	53
Attracting a romantic relationship (2)	17	To clear the air	54
To find a job	18	Attracting prosperity and abundance	55
To purify a place of negative energies and influences	19	To get rid of a bad influence	56
To create opportunities for love	20	To effect a process of reconciliation	57
To cause someone to take the first step	22	Attracting prosperity (2)	58
To extricate yourself delicately from a relationship	23	To bring money into your life	59
Forgetting about an ex-lover	24	To make money using your imagination	60
Reconciliation after a quarrel	26	Recalling loans or debts owed	61
Herbal spells	27	To attain prosperity	62
Reconciliation (2)	28	To obtain the basic things in life	63
Fostering harmony and stopping arguments in a relationship	29	Starting or building up a savings account	64
To bring romance into your life	30	The money box spell	65
Strengthening a marriage	31	New business	66
Using the four elements of nature	32	To fulfill your desires	67
To mend a broken heart	33	Ongoing success in business	68
Recovery from serious illness	34	Finding a new job	69
To thank the divine spirits that guard your home	36	To get the job of your life	70
To bring love into your life	38	To get rid of bad energies	72
Using the ring of protection	39	Passing an exam	73
To find out your lover's initials	40	To enter a state of relaxation	74
To attract a new love into your life	41	To be your own physician	76
Recovery from surgery	42	To get rid of evil intentions	78
General health/healing	43	To make a love potion	79
To send someone a message	44	Gaining confidence and self-esteem	80
Relief of one's own pain	45	Being imbued with courage when facing adversity	81
		Breaking a bad habit	82
		To attract love into your life	84

Breaking a bad habit (2)	85
To make your relationship stronger	86
Developing creativity	87
To reinforce a marriage relationship	88
Attaining happiness	89
Remembering a deceased loved one	
(with more than one person participating)	90
Celebrating the birth or adoption of a child	92
A magic gift for a friend	93
Protecting and purifying your space	94
A blessing for your home	95
Celebrating a wedding or wedding anniversary	96
Consecration of a charm or talisman	98
Making someone think about you	100
The tree of love	101
Releasing the woman inside you	102
Expressing gratitude	103
The moon as a mirror of yourself	104
Protection from abuse	
(when you are the victim)	105
Protection from enemies	106
Protection from gossip or slander	107
Purifying a home (space clearing)	108
Binding love to your life	110
Going back in time	111
Release from negative behaviors or beliefs	112
The sun spell	113
Ending an unwanted relationship or friendship	114
Uniting body, mind and spirit	116
Release from an unwanted suitor	117
Spell for starting the year	118
Release from a hex, curse, or "evil eye"	119
To increase your passion	120
Communication with the spiritual realm	121
A spell for reducing stress	122
Good luck charm	123
Chamomile spell	124
Improving your relationship	126
Egyptian spell	128
Harmony spell	130
The key of life	131
Making a fresh start in life	132
The balloon of success	133
A third wheel	134
To avoid divorce	135
Reinforcing your partner's loyalty	136
Curing depression	137
To conceive a baby son	138
To rid your body of an illness	139
Distance healing	140
Heal your cat	141
Bringing a missing pet back home	142
Prosperity spell	143
Winning the lottery	144
The wishing stone	145
The horseshoe spell	146
The key to a successful life	147
The mother-in-law spell	148
Finding your magic word	149
The justice spell	150
Uniting your family	151
Magnet potion for romance	152
To bring your lover back	153
Spell for "saying without saying"	154
Getting rid of an unwanted lover	155
To conceive a daughter	156
Spell for improving health	157
Improving your eyesight	158
To create a week of wealth	159

Introduction

I write and lecture on subjects connected to Wicca and to good, "white" magic. Everywhere I go, I am asked the same questions: "Can you give us an example of a love spell?" "How can I use magic to get my beloved to come back to me?" "Is there a spell to preserve my youth?" In most of the instances, I promised my readers and audiences that any day now I would be publishing a book on spells.

And I have done it! For two years I read books on spells and magic from around the world, and I corresponded and talked with wizards and witches (most of them female) from all over the world. From each witch I requested their "cream" of all spells — the most common, the most popular, and their favorite spells.

This book includes the most common spells worldwide, and, in fact, the whole range of spells, which answer all the questions asked of witches and wizards.

When performing a spell (there are simple and precise instructions in this book — just like you'd find in a textbook), remember the importance of your intention — you must mean from your heart what you want to achieve from the spell, and that you really want it. This is the first step in achieving a "good" result of a spell.

Let the magic carry you forth,

Tabatha Jennings

spells

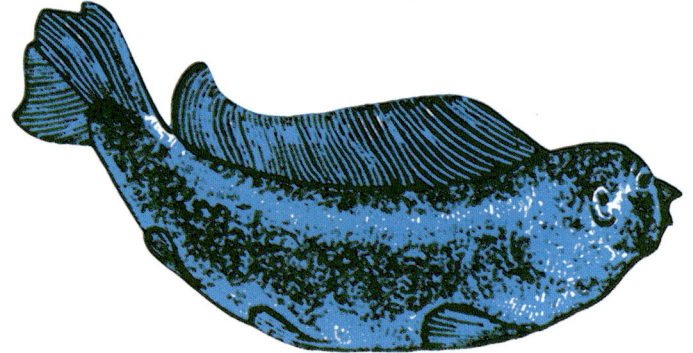

To bring back your lost love

What should you do if you want to bring back your lost love?
You can use this spell to create a relationship between you and the person you believe to be suitable and good for you.
However, in order to use it, you have to understand its symbolism.

This is what you have to do:

1. On a Friday, light blue, red and gold candles. (If you are a woman, light the red candle first; if you are a man, light the blue one first.) Then light the gold candle.
Remember that the gold candle symbolizes a relationship.

2. Place a horseshoe on one side of the candles and a key on the other, and place two roses between them.
Remember that the horseshoe represents luck in love, and the key represents the key to your heart.

spells

3. When the candles burn down, wrap the key, the roses and the horseshoe together in an article of clothing that belongs to the person you love. (If you can't get hold of one, use something of your own.)

4. Place the parcel in one of your bedroom drawers and leave it there for 14 days.

If the roses are still in one piece, it is a good sign. You should bury them together with the horseshoe and the key in a potpourri.

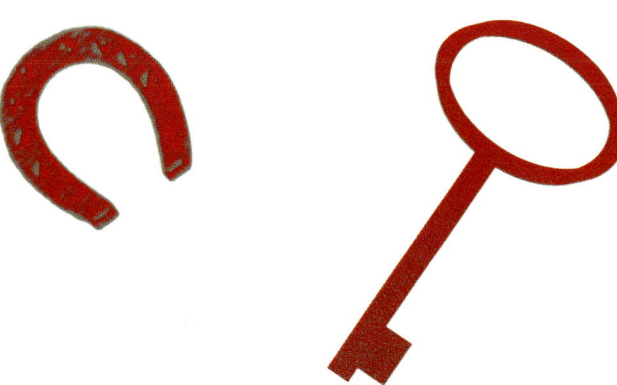

Candle magic rituals for petition

Petition simply refers to asking for something. You might be asking for something to happen or for some type of change or growth to occur.

Asking for something to be removed from your life is also a form of petition.

Candle magic for relationships

Attracting a mate

Rituals for attracting a mate should never be directed at a specific person. Instead, foster the intention of finding a mate with the characteristics you esteem, and concentrate on how you will feel in the new relationship.

Timing Friday, waxing moon cycle or full moon

Candles Your astrological candle or other candle inscribed with your star sign, three pink tapers or small votive candles

Spell

My heart is open,
My love is on the way,
I rise up to greet him/her
As nature greets the day.

Incense Marjoram, rose, or honeysuckle

Crystals Rose quartz, aventurine

Oil Musk

Ritual Light the altar candle. Place the incense next to the altar candle and light it. Place the crystal near the altar candle. Anoint the astrological candle with the oil, working from the wick to the bottom, and place it in front of the altar candle. Anoint the three pink candles and place them in a triangular formation – one on each side of the astrological candle, and one in front of it.

Light the candles beginning with the astrological candle.

Chant the spell. Repeat the spell several times while gazing into the flames. Allow all of the candles to burn down completely.

spells

To find a love partner

What should you do if you are looking for your soul-mate or if your heart is yearning for a real love relationship?

Although this love spell is a little bit complicated because you have to create a protective circle and summon the goddess of love, it will help you find your perfect love partner – not necessarily someone you know.

This is what you have to do:

1. Draw a protective circle, then ground and center yourself in it.

2. Meditate about your ideal partner in order to empty your mind. (Don't think about a specific person. Let your imagination wander, even though you may have a good idea of the qualities you want in your love partner.)

3. Choose a candle in your favorite color. (Be aware that this candle represents you.) As you hold it, meditate and list aloud all of the energies and qualities you would welcome in an intimate relationship.

4. Take a pink cloth and place the candle on it. Put a candle-holder at each end of the cloth.

5. Hold a white candle, which represents your ideal partner, and list aloud the qualities you consider the most important in your partner. Ask the goddess of love, Aphrodite, to help you and your partner get together.

6. Place the two candles in their holders at opposite ends of the cloth.

7. Take a piece of red chalk and draw a heart in the center of the cloth. (Make sure that the heart is big enough for both candle-holders.)

8. Spend a few minutes meditating about your perfect love relationship. Move the two candles a little bit closer together.

9. When the two candles finally meet, draw two more hearts around the first one and let the candles burn down completely.

Alternative for this spell:

Write down a list of all the qualities you want in a partner. While you concentrate intently on your role in the relationship, burn the list and blow the ashes in every direction.
Your wish will soon come true.

Remember! Be careful with both versions, since you might get more than you bargained for.

spells

To increase your attractiveness

According to an old saying, people see you the way you see yourself. If you don't like the image that is reflected in the mirror every day, other people will get the same impression about you, and see you as you see yourself.
This spell is all about changing your attitude toward yourself – first and foremost in your own mind – so that this change will have the same effect on the way other people are attracted to you.

This is what you have to do:

1. As a symbol of new start, clean your bathroom very well, and cover your mirrors with white or pink fabric or towels. Remember, you are creating a new image for yourself, so you shouldn't look at the old one.

2. Fill your bath with hot water. You can light incense if you want.

3. Add a handful of your favorite bath salts or other fragrant substances and say:

I have been renewed from today
My negativity has been washed away
The one I want the most will choose to stay.

4. Light three candles (red, pink and white), and concentrate on the good points of your character.

5. If someone is emerging in your imagination, you can concentrate on him/her, too.

6. Play your favorite music in the background, immerse yourself in the water and relax.

7. Relax in the bath for as long as you can. Every now and then, make sure your body is completely immersed.

8. When you are ready, repeat your opening words. At this point, you can add other things that you feel to be appropriate for these circumstances.

spells

To win someone's heart

To win someone's heart completely in real life can take forever, but when you have succeeded in doing so, you'll realize that it was worth it.
You need a great deal of for this spell. If you lose the impetus for the relationship before you have completed the spell, it may mean that that particular relationship is not right for you.

This is what you have to do:

1. Take a bulb and write the name of the person you love on its base.

2. Plant the bulb in a new flowerpot filled with earth.

3. Place the pot on a windowsill in the direction of your would-be lover's home.

4. Every day and night, stand next to the bulb and repeat the name of the person whose heart you want to win until the bulb takes root, begins to sprout and finally blooms.

5. Repeat the following words every day, filling in the person's name in the last line:

May its roots grow,
May its leaves grow,
May its flowers grow,
And as it does so,
May ......'s love grow.

spells

Attracting a romantic relationship

Timing Monday or Friday, waxing moon cycle

Candles Red seven-day candle, three small votive or straight candles one each in pink, white, and green

Incense Carnation or patchouli

Crystals Rose quartz and lapis lazuli

Herbs Rose petals or basil

Oil Amber, carnation, or gardenia

Spell

I now receive wholeheartedly the new love that is finding his/her way to me now. The rhythm of my heart now matches that of another. I am ready. He/She is here with me. Love is ours.

Ritual Light the altar candle and place the incense beside and light it. Place the herbs on the altar in a small dish or sprinkle them around the altar candle. Place the crystals in front of the altar candle. Anoint the red candle, working from the wick to the end. Place it on the altar. Anoint the green, white, and pink candles and place them in line in front of the red candle. Light the red candle, and then the green, white, and pink candles. Chant the spell. Look into the flames for several minutes while contemplating how you will greet your new love. Allow the candles to burn down.

spells

Attracting a romantic relationship (2)

Timing Three consecutive Fridays, with the last Friday being just before or on the full moon.

Candles One large white pillar candle or three long white tapers; three pink votive candles

Incense Rose

Crystals Rose quartz and green apophyllite

Oil Amber for the white candle, and rose for the pink candles

Spell

A new love is mine, and his path is clear. With sure feet he comes to me as the universe illuminates his path. Closer, closer he draws to my warm embrace. I welcome my new love to my life.

Ritual On the first Friday, light the altar candle and incense, and carve your initials into the white pillar or into one of the white tapers. Anoint the white candle working from wick to end. Anoint one of the pink candles, and place them on the altar, about nine inches apart. Place the rose quartz near the white candle and the apophyllite near the pink candle. Light the candles. Chant your spell several times. If you are using a large pillar candle, snuff it out when the pink candle has burned completely down. If you are using a taper, allow it to burn all the way down. On the second Friday, light the altar candle and incense. Anoint the second pink candle and the second taper (or re-anoint the white pillar), and place them about six inches apart on the altar. Light the candles. Chant your spell several times, and allow the pink candle to burn all the way down. Repeat on the third Friday. This time, if you used a pillar candle, allow it to continue to burn all the way down.

spells

To find a job

If you are looking for a new job but find it difficult to remain focused on your aim and maintain positive energy, this spell will work well for you.

While using it, don't try to imagine specific companies you would like to work for, or other minor details about the job you would like to do, unless you want to utilize particular skills. If you do, it will limit your options to what you want, but will not necessarily offer you what you need or what will be good for you.

This is what you have to do:

(Before starting, you may prepare a list of ads you'd like to reply to.)

1. Hold a crystal or a stone in your hand. The stone represents the job you want. As you hold it, imagine the kind of work you want and the feeling of satisfaction you are yearning for.

2. Speaking aloud, list the qualifications you have for this kind of job.

3. Increase your power by letting your energy build up, flow through you and charge the stone you are holding.

4. The following day, as you contact six potential employers, make sure that you have the stone or crystal with you.

5. Contact exactly six potential employers a day until you get the job you desire.

18

spells

To purify a place of negative energies and influences

If you are buying an old building with the aim of renovating it and converting it into a new house or restaurant, it is highly advisable to use this spell in order to eliminate negative energies and make the place suitable for a different purpose. This spell includes methods taken from Native American rituals and culture, using a smudge stick made of dried herbs.

This is what you have to do:

1. Make a smudge stick out of plants such as sage, cedar, prairie lavender, sweet grass and other dry plants.

2. Light the smudge stick and blow on it until it is burning well. The smudge stick has to remain lit throughout the ceremony.

3. Take the smudge stick and walk in a clockwise direction around the house and then around each room in turn. (Wave the stick around as you walk in order to make sure that the smoke reaches every corner of every room.)

4. Repeat this procedure three times in each room, proclaiming:

I command negativity, fears, problems, habits and bad influences to be gone.

To create opportunities for love

If you want a particular person to be your lover but you are bashful and do not know how to reveal your feelings to him/her, this spell will suit you. Its purpose is to open a path for your love and to send a signal to the person with whom you want to have a relationship.

The spell ensures that there are no delays, but you have to feel something in order for it to work properly.

This is what you have to do:

1. On a Friday night, place a glass of wine on the table.

2. Take a ring (preferably your mother's wedding ring) and make a pendulum by suspending the ring on a red silk ribbon.

3. Resting your elbow on the table, hold the pendulum steady between your thumb and forefinger and let the ring hang over the top of the glass of wine.

4. Utter your name clearly, and then say the name of the person you want.

5. Repeat that person's name twice more (three times in all).

6. Think about the person and spell his name slowly out loud.

7. Before you pronounce each letter of his name, let the ring swing and touch the glass of wine once.

spells

8. Tie the ribbon around your neck so that it hangs over your heart. (In that way, you bring the person you want closer to your heart – both physically and mentally.)

9. Wear this pendulum for three weeks, and repeat the spell every Friday during that time.

When the third week is about to end, the person you wished for in your spell will show an interest in you – unless this love is not meant to be!

spells

To cause someone to take the first step

When you've had a fight or argument with someone you care about, but you have an ego problem when it comes to making the first move toward reconciliation, use this spell to terminate the unpleasant situation. It will cause the other party to make the first move.

This is what you have to do:

1. Choose a night when the moon is waxing, since more energy is available at this time. If you can't wait for the moon to wax, use this spell on any night, but be aware that its effect will not be as powerful.

2. Get a photograph of the person you quarreled with (or some other item that belongs to or represents him/her) and a photograph of yourself.

3. Use a paper clip or something like that to clip the two photographs together.

4. Put them in a dark place, such as at the bottom of a drawer or inside a closet.

5. Leave them there until the person contacts you and responds to the spell.

This spell is more effective if you think about the real reason for your quarrel with this person while you are performing it. It will make you more amenable to shouldering your share of the blame.

spells

To extricate yourself delicately from a relationship

Do you want to terminate a relationship but don't know how to go about it? Are you trying to get rid of a friend who is not good for you anymore?
This spell will help you do it delicately by setting the person free instead of rejecting them.

This is what you have to do:

1. Take a small piece of paper and a black pen (preferably a fountain pen), and write down the name of the person you want to eliminate from your life. When you're through, let the ink dry.

2. Take a white candle and burn the paper, all the while imagining the person leaving you. Make sure to collect the ashes because you will need them later on.

3. Holding the ashes in your right hand, go up to a high place and say:

> Winds of the north, east, south and west,
> Take these ashes to where they will be best.
> Let .....'s heart be open and free,
> Let .....'s mind be far away from me.

4. When you finish declaiming those lines, blow the ashes in the direction of the prevailing wind.

In the hoodoo tradition, you can also dispose of the ashes by throwing them over your shoulder into running water, in the name of the Father, the Son and the Holy Ghost. Then you should walk away and not look back.

spells

Forgetting about an ex-lover

If you have an ex-lover who you just can't get out of your mind, and you feel that this is preventing you from getting involved with other people and finding a new love, this spell is good for you.
It won't help you get rid of the old lover, but it will be helpful in minimizing and clarifying your feelings about him/her and in preparing yourself for a new partner.

This is what you have to do:

1. Take a photograph of your ex-partner and put it in a container. (Make sure that the container is suitable for burning things in.)

2. Set the picture alight inside the container. As it burns, gather up all the pain and hurt that you are feeling.

3. Imagine all these painful feelings dissipating as you declaim these or similar words:

Leave my heart and set me free,
Leave my life without pain for me.
While this picture burns to dust,
Help me move on as I must.

4. Repeat these words until the picture has completely disintegrated.

5. Take the root of woody nightshade (which is poisonous), hold it close to your solar plexus, and let your bad feelings and anger flow into it.

6. Touch your forehead with the root in order to indicate that you have turned your bad feelings into good ones.

7. Wrap everything (including the container of ashes) in a red bag or cloth. As soon as it is convenient for you, bury it as far away from your house as possible.

Don't forget to end the spell by sending loving thoughts to your ex-partner.

spells

Reconciliation after a quarrel

Use this ritual when the party you have quarreled with is not present and/or does not wish to take part in it. Use after quarrels between friends and siblings, as well as between married partners. You can use your own energies to encourage the reconciliation. Repeat the following week if necessary.

Timing Friday, waxing moon cycle or full moon

Spell
We emerge from the dark
All healed, to the light
Distance is banished
Closeness is nigh
Faith rediscovered
Is now within sight
We emerge from the dark
And healed, we face the light

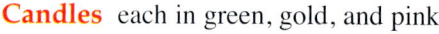

Candles each in green, gold, and pink

Incense Apple or sandalwood

Crystals Lapis lazuli, amethyst, green tourmaline

Herb Yarrow root

Oil Rose

Ritual Light the altar candle. Place the incense near the altar candle and light it. Anoint the two green candles with the oil, working from the wicks to the ends. Place the green candles in front of the altar candle and place the crystals in front of them. Anoint the gold and pink candles, again working from the wicks to the ends. Place the gold candles in front of the green candles and the pink candles in front of the gold. Light the candles, beginning with the green candles. Light the herbs if you wish to burn some. Chant the spell.

spells

Herbal spells

If you have reached the point in your life where you are really looking for true love, don't give up. This spell will help you find your ideal lover.

This is what you have to do:

1. Take a red cloth (red is the color of love) and fill it with rose, passiflora, lavender or jasmine petals. To these, add a red heart and a copper ring.

2. After you've done that, imagine the kind of lover you want in your life. (While doing so, try to clear your mind of other thoughts and concentrate.)

3. Tie up the cloth by winding a blue ribbon (blue is the color of the emotions) around it seven times. While tying it up, you can say out loud:

With these seven ties, I tie my lover to me.

4. Take the cloth bundle, hang it on your bed and wait for the results, which will come soon.

Remember! After doing this, greet every partner who enters your life patiently, because the universe knows who is good for you better than you do.

spells

Reconciliation (2)

This ritual is excellent when both parties wish to take part. It is best for reconciliation between lovers or mates.

Timing Friday, waxing or full moon

Candles Red figure candle depicting embracing lovers, preferably with two wicks, one from each of the figures' heads. One wick is acceptable if it is not from one of the figures' heads, but from a space between them.

Incense Ylang-ylang

Crystals Jade and emerald

Oil Rose

Herb Ginger

Spell

Anger and strife dwell with us no more. Forgiveness rules the day. Embracing we start anew. Our hearts pure and ready we begin again. Love reigns supreme in our dwelling, banishing hurt and resentment. Love, love, is our lot from here forward.

Ritual Light the altar candle and the incense. Carefully and slowly anoint the figure candle, working from wicks to end. If both parties are participating, each should anoint the candle in turn. Then place it in front of the altar candle. Light a small piece of charcoal, and place a tiny amount of dried ginger on the charcoal. Place the crystals near the figure candle, and light the candle. Chant the spell. If both parties are present, each should chant the spell in turn. Allow the figure candle to burn down completely. If it should go out before burning down, consider the ritual done, but incomplete, and repeat the following week with another candle. If the candle burns out leaving a shell of the embracing figures intact, the ritual can be considered finished and complete.

spells

Fostering harmony and stopping arguments in a relationship

Timing Tuesday, during the new or waning moon cycle
Candles Votive candles - one black, one silver, and one indigo
Incense Lilac or lavender
Crystals Clear quartz crystal, green calcite
Oil Amber or lavender

Spell

As these candles banish disharmony and summon peace, so shall it be for all our days. As calm as a lake in morning, and as promising as a rainbow, our bond sways gently in life's breezes. Gently, gently we sway, harmony rules our days.

Ritual Light the altar candle and incense. Anoint the black candle from the end to the wick, and inscribe the names of both parties into the candle. Set the black candle in the center of the altar. Anoint the indigo and silver candles, working from wick to end, and set them one on each side of the black candle. Place the lapis at the base of the silver candle, and the clear crystal between the black and indigo candles. Light the black candle, then the blue and silver candles. Chant the spell. Allow the candles to burn down completely.

spells

To bring romance into your life

If you want to introduce a little romantic love into your life, this spell will do the trick. Be aware that the aim of this spell is to bring love into your life – but not necessarily from the specific person you've set your sights on.

This is what you have to do:

1. Choose a good spot with powerful energies indoors or outdoors. (If you find it difficult to locate this spot, just wander around. When you feel the need to rest, that is the place that contains your powerful energies.)

2. Light a stick of rose incense in order to cleanse both the place and your mind.

3. Take a small box and write on it in red: *This love is mine.*

4. Take a sprig of rosemary and a rose quartz crystal and put them inside the box of love. If you like, you can add anything that reminds you of what love really is for you. (Be careful not to use things that belong to the specific person you want because the aim of this spell is to attract love in general into your life).

5. Light a pink or red candle, clear your mind and imagine yourself very happy and in love. Say:

> *True love is coming to me very soon.*
> *I am surrounded with a white circle of pure, real love.*
> *Love is on its way to me.*

Strengthening a marriage

Timing Friday, waxing moon cycle or full moon

Candles Use two altar candles, two red stick or taper candles, two small yellow votive candles, and two astral candles one for each of the marriage partners.

Incense Sandalwood

Crystals Opal, amethyst, and diamond

Oil Rose

Spell

My love and I are alternately root and tree, tree and root. We support and sustain one another and we each grow our own strong limbs. We face the future as two, and yet as one. We are each happy and powerful in our bond, giving and taking in like portion. Our commitment is strong, our lives joyful.

Ritual Place the two altar candles at the back corners of the altar and light them. Place the incense between the altar candles and light it. Anoint the two red candles, working from the wicks to the center, and then from the center to the bottom. Place the red candles in the center of the altar, slightly in front of the altar candles, with about six inches of space between them. Anoint the astral candles. If they are not already embossed with signs, carve your sign onto the bottom half of one of the astral candles, and that of your partner on the other. You may also carve your names if you wish. Set the astral candles in front of the red candles, about two inches apart. Anoint the yellow candles. Place them in front of the astral candles, about eight inches apart. Light the red candles, and chant your spell. Light the astral candles and repeat the spell. Light the yellow candles and repeat the spell once more.

Allow the candles to burn for a few minutes while you remain with them and concentrate on your desire. Keep the picture of your happy marriage firmly in mind. Next, extinguish the yellow and red candles. Allow the astral candles to continue to burn out completely.

spells

Using the four elements of nature

Sometimes we feel a lack of energy at work, at home and with our friends and family. In order to fortify ourselves, we can use the four elements of nature that surround us all the time: water, air, earth and fire. Those elements were used daily in the ancient Native American culture.

This is what you have to do:

1. Choose a stick of your favorite type of incense (to represent the element of air) and take a white candle. Light them both.

2. While doing so, imagine that you are harnessing the power of the air element and the power of fire element.

3. Summon those elements to come and help you solve whatever problems you are having.

4. Take a bowl, fill it with sand and call upon the power of the earth element for assistance:

I call on the power of earth to help me with ....

5. Take a bowl of water, and call upon the power of the water element for assistance:

I call on the power of water to help me with ....

6. Pour the water into the bowl of sand, bury the ashes of the incense, and douse the candle.

When you have completed this ritual, you will feel strong and full of positive energies, ready to do whatever you felt too weak to do previously.

spells

To mend a broken heart

Our heart is a very important energy center in our body. For that reason, we should listen to it and pay attention to what we allow into it. Every time our heart is broken, it is damaged. This is especially true of a heartbreak caused by love. This spell will help you get the pieces of your heart together and move on.

This is what you have to do:

1. On a Friday morning or evening (Friday is the day of Venus, the goddess of love), light a pink candle and take a bath in salt water.

2. While you are drying yourself, drink strawberry tea and apply strawberry oil or body lotion to your body. (If you are a woman, put on make-up as well, so that you look your best.)

3. Take a willow branch and make a circle around a table containing a pink candle, a mirror, a pink bag, a quartz crystal, a copper penny, a crystal bowl that is special to you, a spoonful of jasmine tea, orris-root, strawberry leaves, yarrow and eight drops of apple oil.

4. Light another pink candle and mix all the oils and herbs together in the bowl. While you are doing so, look at yourself at the mirror.

5. When you are through mixing the ingredients, gaze at yourself in the mirror and say:

Mother of the universe, take all the good in me and help me to be the best person I can be and overcome my difficulty.

6. Put half of the mixture in the pink bag and add the penny and the crystal to it.

7. Carry the bag wherever you go until you no longer feel the need for it.

8. Leave the other half of the mixture in the bowl in your room so that you can smell it.

Repeat this ritual every Friday until you feel better.

spells

Candle magic for physical healing

Recovery from serious illness

Timing Saturday, waning moon cycle

Candles One black candle and an astrological candle representing the person who is ill. Be sure the black candle is not larger or thicker than the astrological candle.

Incense Frankincense, patchouli or sage

Crystals Plain quartz crystal, black onyx. You may add a crystal chosen according to the person's ailment if you wish.

Oil Patchouli

34

Spell

Banish ye illness
Banish ye weakness
Banish ye fear
Banish ye resignation
Healing and light are nigh!
On comes the light!
Illness does not abide the light
And so it retreats
Leaving strength and wholeness
Welcome ye strength and wholeness now!

Ritual Light the altar candle. Place the incense in front of the altar candle and light it. Holding the black candle, carve the sick person's name carefully into the wax. Underneath the name, carve the name of the disease he suffers from. Now anoint the black candle, working from the bottom end up to the wick. Place the black candle in front of the incense. Hold the astrological candle representing the ill person. Carve the patient's initials into the candle, and anoint it working from the wick to the end. Place the astrological candle next to the black candle so that they are touching. Place the crystals near the black candle.

Light the black candle, and then the astrological candle. Leave the candles until the black candle has burned out completely. When the black candle is burned out, extinguish the astrological candle.

spells

To thank the divine spirits that guard your home

Every home has its guardian spirits. If you want to thank the divine spirits for guarding your home, use this spell.

It is best to perform this ritual during the full moon.

This is what you have to do:

1. Choose an appropriate symbol for your guardian spirit and decorate the area around it with green incense and green herbs.

2. Clean the symbol so that it is free of dust.

3. Light the green incense and a green candle.

4. Stand in front of the symbol and say:

I call on the guardian spirits.

I invite you to join me.

You are my friends and I want to thank you for that.

5. Take the incense and walk in a clockwise direction around the symbol three times and say:

Thank you for your help in keeping this house clean, pleasant and peaceful.

6. Carry the candle in a clockwise direction around the symbol three times and say:

Thank you for bringing light to this house and eliminating the darkness.

7. Take a stick that will serve as a magic stick and hold it in your dominant hand. Circle the symbol again in a clockwise direction three times and say:

I seek your protection for me, for my family and for all who live here.
I request that you remove all troubles from this place.
I thank you for your love and understanding.

8. Stand with raised arms and call on your own guardian spirits:

I now call on the guardians of this home to enter my home.
I respect you with this symbol.
I ask your blessing and protection.

Be mindful of changes in the atmosphere. If you feel changes, it is a sign that your guardian spirits have become part of your environment.

This spell will purify your home and the energies in it, and will also help you to keep negative energies away. You can perform it every now and again.

To bring love into your life

The aim of this spell is to bring a new love – not necessarily someone you know – into your life, or to bring a friend of yours closer.

This is what you have to do:

1. On a moonlit night, take an object that comes in pairs such as a pair of shoes or a pot and its lid. Decide which one of them is the "male" and which is the "female."

2. Take a piece of pink ribbon and tie the "female" object to one end of it and the "male" object to the other. (Make sure that there is a good length of ribbon between them.)

3. Each day, bring the two objects a little bit closer, until they are touching.

4. Leave them tied together for a week.

Within a week, a new love should enter your life.

spells

Using the ring of protection

We often feel that people who come to our home bring bad energies with them, causing us to quarrel with our spouse for no real reason. This is the power of bad energies.

By means of this spell, you can protect your home from bad energies and bad spirits, and also protect yourself from those energies prior to going out among people. All you have to do is use your imagination.

This is what you have to do:

1. Imagine a ring of bright and warming light surrounding you (or your home).

2. Ask your guardian spirit to protect you and your house as long as necessary.

Imagine this ring every time you leave your house.

39

To find out your lover's initials

If you are neither married nor in a relationship, but are curious to know the initials of your future partner, use this spell.

This is what you have to do:

1. Take an apple and peel it without allowing the peel to break.

2. Hold the peel in your right hand and say:

I ask the powers of the universe to reveal the first letter of my true love's name.

3. Turn around clockwise three times.

4. Throw the peel over your left shoulder. It will fall in the shape of the first initial of your future lover.

Another version of this spell is to hang the peel in the entrance of your home. The first letter of the name of the first person that enters your home will be the same as that of your future lover.

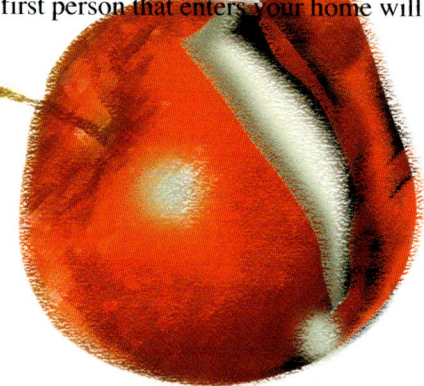

spells

To attract a new love into your life

We all know how hard it is to deal with a broken heart and to find a new love when your heart is still broken. This spell will help you convert your negative energies into positive ones and feel more optimistic about your love life. In order to derive the maximum from it, all the materials you use should be new.

This is what you have to do:

1. Try to choose a time when there is a new moon. If you can't wait for a new moon, the spell will still work, but not quite as effectively.

2. Cut a heart out of a sheet of red paper.

3. Using a new pen, write on a clean sheet of white paper:

*This heart shines with the light of a candle.
Tonight I draw my lover to me.*

4. Take a bath in order to cleanse your body as well as your soul.

5. Light a pink or red candle and read the spell out loud again.

6. Hold the red paper heart in front of the flame and let the candlelight shine through it.

7. Place both the paper you wrote the spell on and the heart in a new envelope.

8. Seal the envelope with candle wax.

9. Hide the envelope somewhere in your room and leave it there for 28 days.

A new love should come into your life by the end of those 28 days.

spells

Recovery from surgery

Timing Tuesday, full or waxing moon

Candles One red figure candle or astrological candle for the recovering patient. One straight or votive candle in each of the following colors: green, orange, white, and red.

Incense Sandalwood

Crystals Carnelian

Herbs Pine

Oil Pine or lilac

Spell

As the universe is a perfect whole, so shall the body strive to become. The body has abilities and powers to heal itself, and these are being put into play now. The healing will be full and complete. Light surrounds the healthy body and glows from the site that is wounded no more.

Ritual Light the altar candle. Place the incense near the altar candle and light it. Hold the figure candle and find the place on it that corresponds to the location of the surgery. Mark the spot on the candle with a small nail or pin. Anoint the other candles from wick to end, and place them around the figure candle, one in each direction. Allow the colored candles to burn down completely. If the figure candle is still burning, light additional colored candles and repeat the spell. Allow the candles to burn down completely.

General health/healing

Timing Sunday, waxing moon cycle

Candles One astrological candle for the person whose health is in question, one small light blue, and one small red candle

Incense Jasmine

Crystal Amber

Oil Gardenia

Herb Pine needles

Spell

The body seeks wholeness
It leans toward the light
Toward abundant strength and fullness
Toward vigor and might
The light enters, and disease flees!
The healing powers have won.

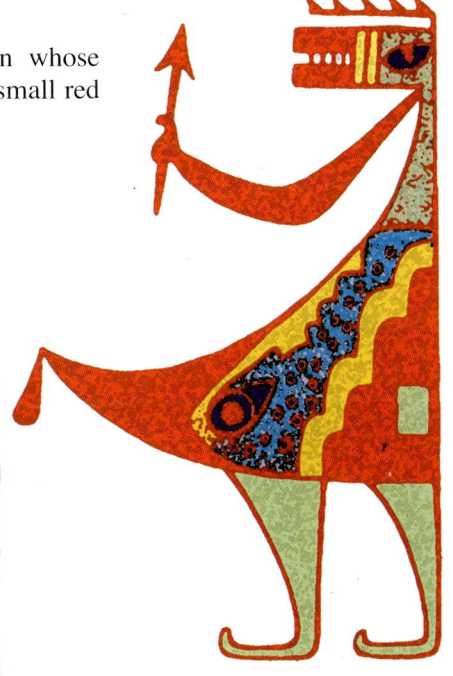

Ritual Light the altar candle and the incense. Etch the sick person's name into the astrological candle (their initials can suffice) and anoint it working from wick to end. Place it in front of the altar candle. Anoint the light blue and red candles and place them on either side of the astrological candle. First light the astrological, then the blue, then the red candle. Place the crystal near the astrological candle. Sprinkle pine needles on the altar. Chant the spell several times. Allow the candles to burn all the way down.

spells

To send someone a message

We often want to tell another person that we are interested in him/her, but somehow fail to get the words out.
This spell will help you send the correct energy to the person you are interested in. It will make him/her aware of you.

This is what you have to do:

You simply have to say:

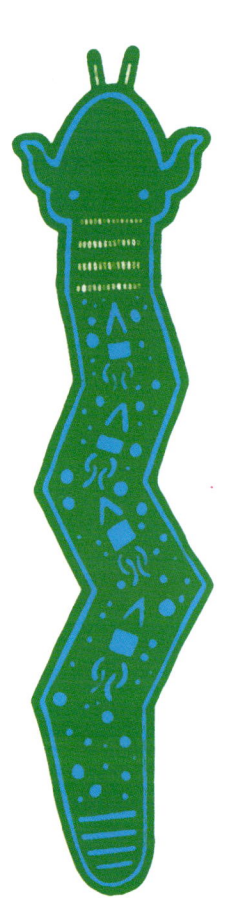

I am coming towards you*
As you are coming towards me.

When I am thinking of you,
You are thinking of me.

I am calling your name
As you are calling to me.

Bring your love to me

* If you know the person's name, say it three times.

You will have to utter this spell a few times until you feel its effect.

44

spells

Relief of one's own pain

Timing Sunday or Wednesday, waxing moon cycle.

Candles One votive candle in each of the following colors: red, white, green, and purple.

Incense Clove

Crystal Aventurine

Oil Juniper

Herb Finely crushed barley

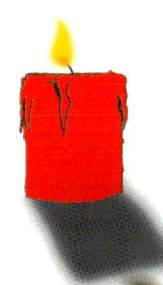

Spell

I release my pain to whence it came
My body is healed, my strength restored
The message of pain was without blame,
Now relief of pain is my reward!
Lesson learned, I onward go Pain free, light as air, in forward flow.

Ritual Light the altar candles and the incense. Anoint the red candle, working from wick to end, being sure to apply a good amount of oil to the base and sides of the candle. Dip or roll the candle in the crushed barley. (Only a small amount need affix itself to the candle). Place the red candle in the center of the altar. Anoint the white, green, and purple candles from wick to end, and place them in front of the red candle. Place the aventurine next to the red candle. Light the red candle, then the white, the green, and the purple. Chant the spell. Allow the candles to burn down completely.

To create a stronger attraction

If you are interested in someone but the other party is not responding to your signals, you can use this spell. It will help you make a direct impression on the person you like. Before using it, however, try to think why the person is ignoring you. You should perform this spell with good clear energies.

This is what you have to do:

1. Light a stick of rose incense.

2. After uttering the name of the person you want, say:

Bring your love to me now.

3. Try to get a few hairs from the person's head and burn them with the incense until they disappear.

4. While the hairs are burning, think about the things that reduce the person's attraction to you. Imagine that those obstacles are turning into passion and love.

spells

To draw your lover's attention to you

If you feel that your partner is not paying enough attention to you, and you want to remind him/her that you are still there, try this spell. It will help you save the energy you are wasting on thinking about it. When you do that, you will automatically feel a change in your lover's attitude.

This is what you have to do:

1. Sit and gaze into a fire inside or outside your house. While doing so, imagine your lover.

2. Using your left hand, throw some laurel leaves into the fire.

3. While the leaves are burning, say:

*During the time those leaves are burning,
The heart I desire is coming to me.*

4. When the fire is put out, utter the spell twice more.

After a day, your lover should begin to change his/her attitude toward you and pay more attention to you.

Candle magic for attracting money and abundance

Money rituals should never be performed when you are feeling frustrated or upset about your situation. Try to release any fears you may have about not having enough. When you are vibrating fear, your magic will not be able to attract abundance, so it is vital that you relax your mind, focus on where you want to be when you have what you desire, and deflect your attention from the actual situation, if it is one of lack. Visualize yourself being able to pay the bills, getting a raise, giving to charity, or whatever your final goal may be, and feel the way you think you will feel when the desire is realized. Then you are ready to perform your ritual and bring what you desire to realization.

Gambling or investment luck

Timing Thursday, full moon

Candles Orange, black, and white

Incense Rose

Crystals Peridot and agate

Herb Mint

Oil Cinnamon

Spell

Money is making its way to me
I feel calm, sustained, and free.
Money quickly fills up my account
Feelings of gratitude abound.

Ritual Light the altar candle and the incense. Anoint the black and orange candles, working from wick to end. Anoint the white candle and carve your initials or astrological sign into the bottom half of the candle. Place the candles on the altar in any formation you like, and place the crystal next to the white candle. Spread mint leaves around the altar. Light the white candle, then the black, and orange. Chant your spell several times and hold the vision of yourself winning or profiting from an investment. Then say, *"I am grateful for what I have received!"* Repeat this several times. Leave the candles to burn down completely.

s p e l l s

To decide between two lovers

Some people have difficulty finding one lover, while others have to decide between two lovers. Which situation is more complicated? There is no correct answer. But if you are in the situation of having to choose between two lovers, this spell may help you, even though it requires a great deal of patience.

This is what you have to do:

1. Using a new pin, etch the name of your first lover onto a bulb.

2. Using another pin, etch the name of your second lover onto another bulb.

3. Plant the two bulbs next to each other in the ground, and remember which name is written on each one.

4. The bulb that sprouts first symbolizes the better option out of your two lovers.

Remember! You need a lot of patience to wait for the bulbs to sprout. That being the case, your problem might well resolve itself even before the spell has been completed.

spells

Attracting fast money for a specific purpose

If you are presented with an unexpected large bill, incur a sudden expense due to accident or illness, or need to help a child or friend and don't have the funds, this type of ritual can help attract a specific sum of money quickly.

Timing Sunday, full or waxing moon

Candles Astrological candle for the person in need of the money, and one brown, one gold, and one green candle

Incense Cinnamon

Crystals Garnet, aventurine, citrine

Oil Jasmine

Other Small sheet of brown paper

Spell

Money is making its way to me
I feel calm, sustained, and free.
Money quickly fills up my account
Feelings of gratitude abound.

Ritual Light the altar candle and incense. Anoint the brown candle, working from the wick to the end, and inscribe it with a dollar sign or the words "fast money." On the sheet of brown paper, write down the exact sum of money that will meet your immediate needs. Place the brown candle on the altar in front of the incense. Anoint the other candles from wick to end, and place your astrological candle very close to the brown candle, just behind it. Place the gold and green candles on either side of the astrological candle. Place your crystals in front of the candles. Light the candles. Chant your spell several times. Allow the candles to burn down completely.

spells

To clear the air

Many people find themselves in situations in which there is a lack of communication between them and their lovers or partners. In most cases, each of the partners has an ego problem that does not permit a new line of communication to be opened.

This spell will help you open up a new and effective line of communication with your partner.

This is what you have to do:

1. Take a magnifying glass and place it over a photograph of your partner's face.

2. While looking at the magnifying glass, list all the difficulties you are experiencing, and what you would like your lover to do about them.

In a few hours, your partner will receive your message, and a new line of communication open up for both of you.

Attracting prosperity and abundance

Magic to attract prosperity will be more powerful if combined with a belief that you are worthy and deserving of abundance in life. Be sure your spell includes an affirmation that you deserve what you are asking for. If you do not feel that you do, your own vibrations of unworthiness will be counterproductive, and the magic will not be successful. Check your beliefs and try to align them with your desires before attempting the magic.

As you gain more prosperity, perform periodic rituals affirming this success and asking for its continuation.

Timing Thursday, full or waxing moon

Candles One green or white seven-day glass-encased candle and 28 orange votive candles. Use two large altar candles to anchor a strong energy.

Incense Bayberry

Crystals Malachite and citrine

Oil Bergamot

Spell
A deserving soul am I, and good!
All I wish comes to me and well it should.
Abundance and fortune will now be mine,
Prosperity is right for me, in space and time.

Ritual Light the altar candles at the back of each end of the altar. Anoint the exposed wax of the seven-day candle and place it in the center of the altar. Anoint the orange candles, working from the wick to the end, and place two on each side of the seven-day candle. Place the crystals among the candles. Light the seven-day candle, and then the orange candles. Chant the spell several times. Allow the orange candles to burn all the way down on the first day, while leaving the seven-day and altar candles lit. Each day for the seven days, light another four orange candles, and chant the spell several times. Allow the seven-day candle to burn down completely.

spells

To get rid of a bad influence

Sometimes there are people who have a bad influence on us. Those people can even convince us to do something we don't really want to do. Usually, we react angrily to this and we feel bad about it.
This spell will help you get rid of this anger.

This is what you have to do:

1. Choose a night when the moon is waning and make a fire.

2. Go out and collect vervain leaves. While you are doing that, shout out the name of the person who caused you to feel the anger.

3. Throw the leaves into the fire and say loudly and passionately:

I request that you leave me now.
I don't need you in my life.

Be aware of the fact that this spell can get this person out of your life for good, so don't use it on every person who makes you angry. Save it for real anger.

To effect a process of reconciliation

Many people reach the point of a rift in their marriage. Some people decide to throw in the towel, while others opt to mend the rift.
This spell can help you begin a process of reconciliation with your partner.

This is what you have to do:

1. Cut an apple in half. Try to keep the seeds intact.

2. Write your name on a sheet of paper and next to it write the name of your spouse or any other partner on whom you wish to put the spell.

3. Cut out the names that you have written.

4. Place the names between the two apple halves.

5. While doing so, imagine that the relationship is thriving.

6. Use two pins to stick the apple halves together from right to left and vice versa.

7. When you have done that, send love and good energies to the person you love, and ask for their love and good energies in return.

Attracting prosperity (2)

Timing – Thursday, waxing or full moon

Candles – Five green and one yellow votive candles; one astrological candle to represent the person who wishes for prosperity

Incense – Lavender or patchouli

Crystals – Citrine, malachite

Oil – Peppermint

Spell

Oh abundant universe, rich in all, send me what is mine! I attract a full portion. May I take part in the fullness of thy supply. Fortune now rains on me, and prosper I will! How grateful am I for the abundance that is mine!

Ritual – Light the altar candle and incense. Place the crystals in front of the altar candle. Anoint the astrological candle working from wick to end, and place it in front of the crystals. Anoint the green candles and place them in a line in front of the astrological candle. Anoint the yellow and candle and place it in front of the green candles. Light the candles, working from back to front. After the yellow candle is lit, chant the spell several times. Allow all of the candles to burn down completely.

spells

To bring money into your life

Money is one of the few things in life that, no matter how much you have, it's never enough.
This spell will help you bring more money into your life. However, always remember that money is only the means to accomplish your goals, and not the goal itself.

This is what you have to do:

1. Choose an open place outdoors on a night when there is a full moon.

2. Look at the moon. While doing so, take your wallet and turn your money over three times.

3. Look at the moon again and say:

I request that the universe bring me a fortune with love and good energies. I promise to use this money for good purposes.

You know that the spell has worked if there is more money in your purse, if you find money somewhere in the street, or if money reaches you in any other way.

spells

To make money using your imagination

We all spend a lot of time thinking about how to make more money so that we can live in the way we want and do the things we enjoy doing. It did not occur to anybody to do this using only our imagination and a few other tools.

This spell will help you bring more money into your life. In order for it to succeed, you have to use your imagination effectively.

This is what you have to do:

1. Make a bag from a piece of fabric.

2. When the bag is ready, meditate for an hour, using your imagination. This means that you should sit comfortably and imagine how money comes to you and what you do with it. While doing so, think about the small details.

3. Take three silver coins, breathe on them three times and say:

I call on the power of the universe to bring money into my life.

4. Take an old piece of cloth and place the following items in it: a piece of yellow fabric, a few herbs such as saffron or lavender, a crystal, gold and silver wire and the three silver coins.

5. Place the cloth in the bag you prepared beforehand, and close the bag with eight loops (the number eight symbolizes spiritual and material success).

6. Put the bag in a cool, dark place in your home for eight days.

After that time, you should receive money.

Recalling loans or debts owed

Before attempting to use magic to influence clients to pay what they owe you, or friends to repay a loan, be sure to let go of any anger you may have surrounding this debt. If you need to, use a magic ritual for the release of anger and animosity first. Incorporate into your spell the belief that from now on you will always be paid on time. Do not mention a specific person's name in your magic spell.

Timing – Saturday, during the full or waxing moon.

Candles – One yellow and one green

Incense – Jasmine

Crystals – Amber, topaz, emerald

Oil – Orange

Herbs – Nutmeg, honeysuckle

Other – Sheet of green paper, metal or glass bowl

Spell

I open myself to what is mine. I attract it unto me in timely manner Bring me what is mine, no less! As I have given, so I shall receive.

Ritual – Light the altar candle and the incense. Place the crystals at the front of the altar. On the sheet of green paper, write the amount owed to you if it is a specific debt you wish repaid. If you wish to initiate a general pattern of being paid in a timely manner by clients, write the statement: "My clients always pay me happily and on time. What they owe me will be paid quickly and soon." Place the paper on the altar, underneath one of the crystals. Anoint the candles, working from wick to end, and place them in the center of the altar. Light the candles, first the green and then the yellow. Take the sheet of paper, fold it several times, and using the flame of the green candle, set it on fire, and gently place it in the bowl. As it burns, chant your spell. Allow the candles to burn down completely.

spells

To attain prosperity

This spell can help alleviate money worries and bring money into your life.

This is what you have to do:

1. Place a small bowl and a yellow candle on a table or any other place where you can see them every day.

2. Each day for seven days, place a coin in the bowl until there are seven coins in it.

3. At the end of the seven days, hold the candle in your hand and imagine yourself attaining happiness, wealth and prosperity via the candle. Think about all the good things you are going to do with the money.

4. Replace the candle and take the seven coins in your left hand.

5. Arrange the coins in a circle around the candle.

6. Place the first coin close to the candle and say:

Money is coming to me soon,
Money is coming to me soon and it is mine.

spells

To obtain the basic things in life

Some people are content with the basic things in life, such as food and a roof over their heads. It is human nature to want more than you have, but if you have reached the point that the basic things in life are the things that are important to you, this spell will help ensure that you will always have them.

This is what you have to do:

1. Place two spoons of rice, sugar and salt in a bowl.

2. Place an open safety pin and in the center of the bowl.

3. Place the bowl outside, in an open place.

4. When you feel that the time is right, replace the ingredients in the bowl with fresh ones.

When you have done this, you will feel that even if your financial situation is difficult, you will somehow always have the basic things you need to survive.

spells

Starting or building up a savings account

Timing – Seven consecutive days during the waxing moon cycle, beginning or ending on a Thursday

Candles – Seven green straight or votive candles

Incense – Ginger

Crystals – Lodestone and citrine

Oil – Bergamot

Other – Several Chinese coins or coins of your country's currency

Spell

As the sapling grows into a tree, so my money takes root and flourishes. Each penny to a dollar grows and so it goes and goes and goes. As I decree so shall it be.

Ritual – Perform this ritual each day for seven days in a row. On each subsequent day, light the altar candle and incense, and place the lodestone and citrine in front of the incense burner. Anoint one of the green candles and place it in front of the crystals. Place the coins at the base of the candle, or under the lodestone. Light the green candle, and chant the spell several times. Allow the candle to burn down completely. Remove the coins and the other articles and begin each day with a clean and fresh altar. Repeat the ritual, using a new set of coins each day, adding them to the ones from the previous day(s). At the end of the seven days, place the lodestone and all of the coins used in the ritual in a box or drawer for several weeks.

The money box spell

Use this spell to attract money or find a good job that will provide you with more money. The spell originates from the voodoo culture.

This is what you have to do:

1. Take a box and place the following items in it: three cinnamon sticks, three kernels of dried corn, three seeds of wheat, three coins, three sesame seeds and three pecans.

2. Close the box tightly and shake it in order to mix all the ingredients together. Say the following words several times:

With these words, I call on the power of good spirits to send me money and a good job.

3. Take the box and bury it near your home.

4. Put your old wallet next to it. (If you leave the box in your home, put the wallet next to it.)

Soon you will receive money or get a better job.

spells

To get the job of your life

If there is a job you really want, a job that suits your talents and your inclinations, a job you feel was tailor-made for you, this spell can help you by giving you all the strength you need to get it.

This is what you have to do:

1. Light a stick of cinnamon incense. (This symbolizes prosperity).

2. Take two brown candles, one green candle, and another candle in a color that is significant for you.

3. Spread olive oil all over the candles, from top to bottom.

4. Place the two brown candles in the center of the table. Place the green candle to their left and the candle you chose to their right.

5. Light your candle and say:

I ask the white spirits to open up my path and to bring the right job for me.

6. Light the green candle and say:

I summon my good luck to come to me.

7. Light the brown candles and say:

The path to the job I desire is already on its way to me.

8. Let the candles burn down.

<u>Remember</u>! Fire is the symbol of the power that drives us forward in life.

spells

To enter a state of relaxation

This ritual is good when you need to enter a meditative state in order to think clearly about your feelings, plans or anything else for which you need a clear mind. It will help you access your inner being in the best way.

This is what you have to do:

1. Choose a night when there is a new moon.

2. Cut a circle the size of your mirror from a sheet of white paper.

3. Cover your mirror with the white circle of paper.

4. Place a thin white candle on the right side of the mirror and light it.

5. Light a stick of incense and say:

*Nocturnal power of the universe,
I am calling on you tonight in this ritual and asking for your spiritual blessing.*

spells

6. Remove the white paper from the mirror, and when you see the reflection of the moonlight in the mirror say:

I thank the light of the moon for shining my way.
I honor and bless you.
I ask you to help me understand the things I feel and think inside.
Let your light reveal the knowledge you have
So I will know how to act in the way that is right for me.

7. Let the candle burn down while you are thinking deeply about the things that are running through your mind and your heart.

spells

To be your own physician

Most illnesses originate from both body and soul. This means that your body's reactions are direct consequences of the way you feel. If you think positively, no illness will want to reside in your body, and vice versa.
So always try to think and act positively. If, however, you fail to do that and contract some kind of illness as a result, use this spell.

This is what you have to do:

1. Take a thin rope and mark off six equal parts.

spells

2. Make five loops over the marks and say aloud:

I am healthy.
I ask the illness to leave my body.
It is time for you to go away.
I call on all the organs of my body to help get the illness out of me.
By means of these words, the illness will depart.

3. Fill a box with sand.

4. Put the rope in the box, seal it properly and bury it.

The next morning, get up feeling healthy. If you feel that you are not yet strong enough,

To get rid of evil intentions

Sometimes we feel bad energies and evil intentions emanating from people. This can be the result of something that has been said or done to us. Use this ritual to cleanse your aura.

This is what you have to do:

1. Bury a piece of string in the ground. (Mark the place so you will remember where it is.)

2. Two days later, dig it up.

3. Place a bottle on the ground, tie the string around it with one knot and say:

I am burying these bad energies deep in the ground and I am cleansing my aura of these negative intentions.

4. Close the bottle and bury it.

This spell will fortify you against another person's evil intentions.

To make a love potion

If you have a date with someone you really want as a lover, and you want to intensify the relationship, use this love potion.

This is what you have to do:

1. Mix five drops each of rosemary oil, lemon oil and rosewood oil together.

2. Spread the oil of love you have prepared over a red candle.

3. One hour before your date is due to arrive, light the candle.

This date will be different. Soon you will feel the relationship becoming stronger.

Candle magic for personal growth

Gaining confidence and self-esteem

Timing – Thursday, full or waxing moon

Candles – One tall yellow taper or other yellow candle, one silver votive and one purple votive (be sure the taper is large enough not to burn down before the votives; a small yellow pillar or other yellow candle can be substituted)

Incense – Carnation

Crystals – Hematite, red jasper, chalcedony

Oil – Ginger

Spell

My personal power knows no limit. I am a limitless being, deserving of all kindness, respect, and grace. Courageous I stand, knowing full well my worth and strength.

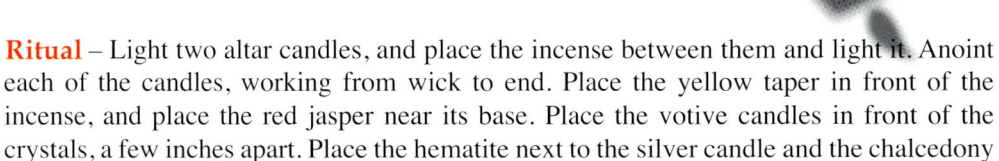

Ritual – Light two altar candles, and place the incense between them and light it. Anoint each of the candles, working from wick to end. Place the yellow taper in front of the incense, and place the red jasper near its base. Place the votive candles in front of the crystals, a few inches apart. Place the hematite next to the silver candle and the chalcedony next to the purple candle. Light the candles, first the yellow, then the silver and purple. Chant your spell, while picturing yourself in a situation where greater self-esteem will be of benefit to you. Picture your "ideal self" behaving and reacting in the situation. Chant your spell again. Allow the candles to burn down completely.

Being imbued with courage when facing adversity

Timing – Saturday, full or waxing moon

Candles – One red, one orange, and one gold; votives or small straight or tapered candles may be used.

Incense – Musk

Crystals – Tiger's eye and aquamarine

Oil – Yarrow

Spell

My eyes are open
My steps are sure
Nothing shall deter me
My intentions are pure
Onward I march
Knowing not fear
My heart is courageous
The ring of victory I hear!

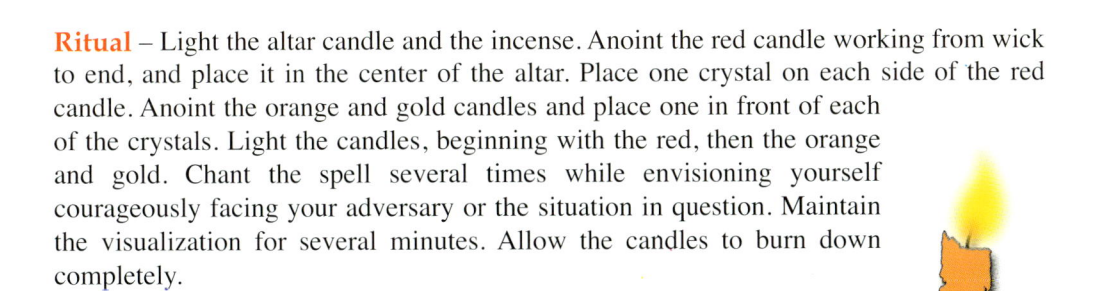

Ritual – Light the altar candle and the incense. Anoint the red candle working from wick to end, and place it in the center of the altar. Place one crystal on each side of the red candle. Anoint the orange and gold candles and place one in front of each of the crystals. Light the candles, beginning with the red, then the orange and gold. Chant the spell several times while envisioning yourself courageously facing your adversary or the situation in question. Maintain the visualization for several minutes. Allow the candles to burn down completely.

spells

Breaking a bad habit

In order to break a bad habit, two types of change have to occur. First, the habit must be banished or distanced from your range of desire. And second, in order to keep it at bay, a positive new behavior or thought process must replace the habit. It is advisable to perform two separate rituals. One will be a banishing ritual, and the other an acquisition ritual. It is vital that you be able to visualize yourself both without the bad habit and with the new behavior. Practice these visualizations for several days before attempting the magic rituals.

Be aware that you can not banish a habit from someone else, but only from yourself.

Timing – Tuesday, full or waning moon

Candles – One straight orange candle and one straight black candle

Incense – Cedar

Crystal – Jade

Oil – Clove

Herb – Rue

Other – Sheet of black paper and white paint or ink. Small charcoal block and heat-resistant bowl for burning the herb.

spells

Ritual – Light the altar candle. Light the incense. Anoint the black candle, working from the end toward the wick. With a small nail or blade, inscribe the black candle with a symbol or word depicting the habit you wish to break.

Place the black candle in the center of the altar. On the black paper, use the white ink to inscribe the sentence: "I release my desire for/to _____." Fold the paper several times and place it under the black candle. Anoint the orange candle, working form the wick to the end, and place it to the left of the black candle. Place the jade crystal in front of the orange candle. Light the charcoal, and place a small amount of rue on it. Wait until it begins to smoke and spread the smoke around the altar.

Light the black candle, then the orange. Recite the spell while maintaining the vision of yourself banishing the bad habit and mentally forming a shield between you and the habit. Chant the spell eight more times. Leave the candles to burn down completely.

Spell

I hereby banish from my desire for/to _____. I see it retreat into the distance as a vague memory of my past. I was weak but now am strong. I was misguided and now am wise. I release my need and desire for _____ to the universe. There is no path for its return to me. I am grateful to be without it, and calmly move forward as it remains behind.

To attract love into your life

If you want to attract the love of someone you know into your life, use this spell.

This is what you have to do:

1. Mix four drops each of ylang-ylang oil, sandalwood oil and rosemary oil together.

2. Spread the mixture of oils over a red candle.

3. Let the candle burn daily for three hours a day until you see some progress in the way your desired partner behaves toward you.

Breaking a bad habit (2)

Note that the previous ritual should be performed during the waning moon cycle, and this ritual should be performed as soon as possible afterwards, when the moon is begins to wax.

Before beginning this ritual, bear firmly in mind the new behavior or thought pattern with which you are replacing your bad habit. Be sure you feel happy and comfortable when performing the new action, so that you can visualize it strongly.

Timing – Thursday, waxing moon

Candles – Green, yellow, and white taper or straight candles

Incense – Rosemary

Crystals – Sodalite

Oil – Peppermint

Herbs – Dragon's blood

Other – Small charcoal block and heat resistant bowl for burning herbs.

Spell

I renew myself now and dedicate myself to change. With joy and strength I walk my new path. I become the new and the new becomes me.

Ritual – Light the altar candle and incense. Light the charcoal block and when it glows add a small amount of dragon's blood. When the herb begins to smoke, lift the bowl and pass the smoke around the altar. Place the bowl near the altar candle and allow the herb to finish burning. More can be added as it burns away. Anoint the green and yellow candles, working from wick to end. Place them side by side in front of the burning herb. Anoint the white candle, and place it, centered, in front of the other candles. Place the sodalite at the base of the white candle. Light the candles, first the green, then the yellow and white. Recite the spell several times, envisioning yourself having adopted the new behavior and feeling happy and relaxed. Allow the candles to burn down completely.

To make your relationship stronger

Use this spell to make your relationship stronger.

This is what you have to do:

Mix ten drops each of lavender oil, sandalwood oil and rose oil together.

This mixture can serve as a perfume or as an air-freshening fragrance. Use it as much as you can in your home and soon your attitude toward your relationship will change.

Developing creativity

Timing – Wednesday, full or waxing moon

Candles – Straight candles, one each in yellow and orange

Incense – Lotus

Crystals – Chrysolite and chrysoprase

Oil – Peppermint

Spell

Ideas originate in my fertile mind. Joyously I bring them to fruition. I create with ease and joy, as the new and fresh come to me and through me.

Ritual – Light the altar candle and the incense. Anoint the yellow candle working from wick to end. Place it in the center of the altar, and place the chrysolite next to its base. Anoint the orange candle and place it next to the yellow one, with the chrysolite near its base. Light the candles. Chant the spell while nurturing a light and joyous emotion in your heart. Envision a white light surrounding the candles and your altar. Remain calm and serene, with an open feeling. Allow the candles to burn down completely.

spells

To reinforce a marriage relationship

If you want to reinforce your marriage, whether it is good or bad, this oil spell will help you. It can also help you direct a relationship toward marriage.

This is what you have to do:

1. Mix two drops of sandalwood, two drops of cypress oil and four drops of lemon oil together.

2. Spread the marriage oil over a pink candle when you are with your partner.

3. Light the candle. Allow the candle to burn down completely.

Now you just have to be patient and start imagining your wedding outfit!

Attaining happiness

Timing – Friday, full or waxing moon

Candles – One tall gold taper, one tall light blue taper, and one pink votive or short pillar candle

Incense – Gardenia

Crystal – Amethyst

Oil – Amber

Other – Several flower heads from pink, yellow and white flowers such as roses or carnations; a plate or a saucer

Spell

I make the choice, out loud, and clear
Only happy sounds I choose to hear
I make the choice, for it is right
Only to see the happy sights
I make the choice, with a nod and a wink
From now only happy thoughts shall I think.
For the choice IS mine, and I believe,
My world shall be AS I PERCEIVE!

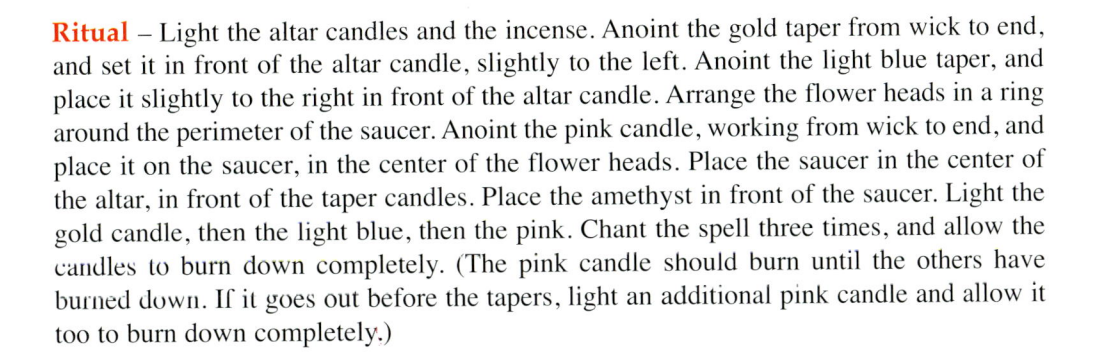

Ritual – Light the altar candles and the incense. Anoint the gold taper from wick to end, and set it in front of the altar candle, slightly to the left. Anoint the light blue taper, and place it slightly to the right in front of the altar candle. Arrange the flower heads in a ring around the perimeter of the saucer. Anoint the pink candle, working from wick to end, and place it on the saucer, in the center of the flower heads. Place the saucer in the center of the altar, in front of the taper candles. Place the amethyst in front of the saucer. Light the gold candle, then the light blue, then the pink. Chant the spell three times, and allow the candles to burn down completely. (The pink candle should burn until the others have burned down. If it goes out before the tapers, light an additional pink candle and allow it too to burn down completely.)

spells

Candle magic for consecration, memorial, and celebration

Remembering a deceased loved one (with more than one person participating)

This ritual can be performed on the loved one's birthday, on memorial days that are predetermined by your religion, or on holidays when the family is together and is acutely feeling the loss of the missing person.

Timing – Birthday of deceased, anniversary of death, religious memorial day or any other day when the loved ones of the deceased are gathered. Preferably but not necessarily during waxing moon cycle.

Candles – One white or purple glass-encased candle (can be seven-day candle if desired); one white straight or taper candle or white votive candle for each person taking part.

Incense – Patchouli or frankincense

Crystals – Two or more large clear quartz crystals with large points

Oil – Lotus

Other – Photo of deceased in which he or she appears alone, and another where he or she appears with one or more of the people present. The photos should be in frames that can stand on a table-top.

For this ritual you may chant a prayer for the dead that is particular to your religion, or read a passage that was meaningful to the deceased, or that appeals to the person leading the ritual. After this, chant the following:

Spell

Safe in our hearts, and joined with our souls, your memory remains. You now travel in realms we have forgotten but will come to know again. With gratitude for what we gained by our bond with you in this world, we release you yet retain your memory with love. May your soul continue to grow and flourish.

Ritual – Light two large altar candles in each of the back corners of the altar. Light the incense and pass it among the participants. Place the incense between the altar candles. Anoint the exposed wax of the memorial candle, working in a clockwise direction, and place it in front of the incense, in the center of the altar. Place the crystals next to the memorial candle. Arrange the holders for the white candles around the memorial candle. Anoint the white candles one by one, working from the wick to the end. As each candle is anointed, hand it to one of the participants. Taking the last anointed white candle, light it in the flame of one of the altar candles. Light the memorial candle with the flame of your white candle. Say the first part of the spell (prayer or other portion) while holding your white candle. Now light each of the participants' candles in turn, beginning with the candles of children if there are any, from youngest to eldest. Each participant should place his own candle in a holder. When all of the white candles have been lit and placed, chant the second part of the spell. After a moment of silence, allow each participant to speak about the deceased and their positive memories, if they so wish. Allow the white candles to burn down completely. Extinguish the altar candles, and allow the memorial candle to burn down completely.

spells

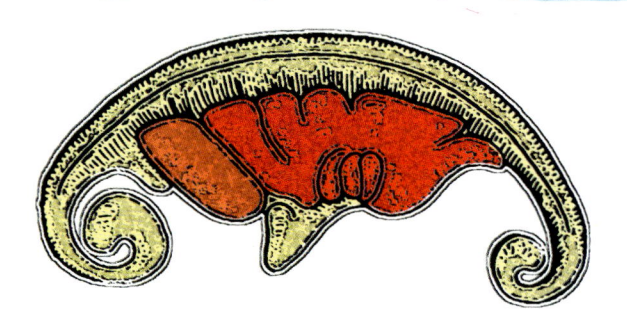

Celebrating the birth or adoption of a child

Timing – Monday, full or waxing moon

Candles One straight or tapered candle in each of the following colors: white, gold, yellow, green, and pink; one straight candle in the child's zodiac color

Spell

Welcome the new child to this realm of joy. May you proceed with your chosen lessons in this world with sureness of purpose and lightness of mind. May the pure light of happiness always shine upon you. May you always choose the path of goodness, strength, and prosperity. Love surrounds you this day, as evermore.

Incense – Rose or mint

Crystal – Rose quartz

Oil – The child's zodiac oil

Other – Small sheet of white paper and a pen with ink in the child's zodiac color.

Ritual – Light the altar candle and the incense. Anoint the straight candles working from wick to end, and place them in a straight line front of the incense, with the child's astrological candle on the far right, then the white, gold, yellow, green and pink candles. Write the child's full name on the sheet of paper, and fold it several times. Place the folded paper in front of the child's astrological candle, and place the crystal on the paper. Light the astrological candle, and then the other candles, from left to right. Chant the spell. Allow the candles to burn down completely.

A magic gift for a friend

If you want to give one of your friends a gift and wish to add magic power to it, use this spell. It will help you increase the power of the object you want to give, thereby creating a significant gift with your own power.

This is what you have to do:

1. Hold the gift you want to give in your dominant hand.

2. Call on the goddess of love by saying: "I call on all my good powers to enter this object I am holding."

3. Feel the energy flowing from your hand, through your body, into the object with wishes of health, love and happiness.

4. When you are through, and you feel that the object is charged with your good energies, wrap it up and say: "I send you health, love and happiness with all my heart and all my powers."

Protecting and purifying your space

If you want to purify and protect a particular room from bad energy, this spell will help you. With this spell, you avail yourself of the highest authority of protection, the authority that contains all the elements of nature. This ritual is taken from the Kabbala.

This is what you have to do:

1. Stand inside the room you want to purify and request the assistance of the power of the universe.

2. Walk in a circle around the room three times.

3. When you have done that, come to a halt facing east.

4. Place two fingers of your right hand on your third eye (in the middle of your forehead) and imagine white light entering the third eye, where your fingers are.

5. Now place your hand on your solar plexus. Concentrate and imagine the white light becoming wider as it moves down toward your feet. Say: *"Malkut."*

6. Move your hand to your right shoulder, imagining that the light is following you, and say: *"Ve gvura."*

7. Move your hand across your chest to your left shoulder, touch it and say: *"Ve hesed."*

8. Clasp your hands and place them in the center of your chest, imagining that the light is following you there, and say: "I call on God to help me purify this place of bad energies, and I call on God to protect me from them. Amen."

A blessing for your home

Our home is our sanctuary. It is a very important place for replenishing our energies. Anything that happens outside our home can affect us, and that is why we have to make sure that when we go back home, it is a relaxed place with good energies – a place where we can become stronger. If you want to bless your home with good and pure energies, this spell can help you.

This is what you have to do:

1. Take a crystal, and hold it in both hands.

2. Imagine that your power is flowing from you into the crystal. Continue for a few minutes.

3. Ask for a blessing and good energies to come into your home.

4. When you are through, put the crystal in a place where it can be seen when someone enters your home.

The crystal will safeguard the energies of the home. If bad energy should enter, the crystal will absorb it. This is why you should cleanse the crystal by placing it in the sun for half an hour every now and then.

Celebrating a wedding or wedding anniversary

This ritual is for the couple to perform together, along with friends or family if desired.

Timing This ritual can be performed on the day before the wedding, and up to one week following the wedding. If it is an anniversary, perform the ritual on the anniversary itself.

Candles Two pink straight or tapered candles, one gold votive and one green votive

Crystals Rose quartz (large unpolished piece), and clear quartz crystal

Incense Frankincense

Oil Rose

Other Wedding rings or other gifts given each to the other. Small vase with twelve pink or white flowers, or small saucer with 12 pink or white flower heads arranged on it. White lace doily or other small decorative cloth.

White sheet of paper, and two pens, each with colored ink appropriate to the astrological sign of one of the partners.

Ritual – Light the altar candle and the incense. Place the flowers in the center of the altar. Anoint the pink candles, working from the wick to the end, and place them side by side about a half-inch apart, behind the flowers. Place the rings or gifts on the doily in front of the flowers. Write the full names of the members of the couple on the white paper, each in his or her own astrological color. If the ritual takes place before the wedding and the bride will be changing her name, use the name she will be taking. Fold the paper once, and place it under the flowers. Place the quartz crystal to the right of the pink candle on your right, and the rose quartz to the left of the pink candle on your left. Anoint the green and gold votives working from wick to end, and place them in front of the gifts.

Light the pink candles, then the green and gold candles. Chant the spell. Allow the candles to burn down completely.

Spell

Our love is a golden light that surrounds us, and a white light within us. Our love is healthy, and our love is strong. Our love is a bond yet we are not bound. Understanding guides our steps, and wisdom guides us to understanding. In rhythm with our higher selves we seek what life has to offer, and offer to it our best, individually and together. May we seek to be joyous individuals, and thus afford one another a clearer path to joy.

Consecration of a charm or talisman

An object can never in and of itself provide us with "luck." We make our own reality and the events of our lives follow our train of thought. However, we can infuse and charge objects with our thoughts and vibrations, thus making them powerful "carriers" of our intentions and desires. An object thus charged, especially if the object itself carries some intrinsic meaning for its owner, can be used as a talisman, or "good luck charm." The talisman can be a piece of special jewelry, a watch, a crystal, or any other object which can be safely carried at all times and is a convenient size to keep in pocket or purse.

It is a good idea to be sure the talisman is waterproof and fairly durable. Use the following ritual to charge the talisman, in a similar manner to the programming of crystals discussed earlier.

Timing – Monday, full or waxing moon

Candles – One red and one black straight or votive candle

Incense – Lotus or frankincense

Crystals – Bloodstone and black obsidian or black onyx

Oil – Myrrh or lotus

Other – The object you wish to consecrate as a talisman

Ritual – Light the altar candle and the incense. Anoint the black candle, working from the end to the wick while maintaining the intention to banish bad decision and blunders from your life. Anoint the red candle working from the end to the wick while maintaining the intention to bring joy and luck into your life.

Spell

When you are near, I am protected. When you are near my aura is strong and bright. Keeping you near, I intensify my intention for joy and good fortune shall be mine. My steps will be wisely guided by my highest self, as long as you are in my possession. From this moment I consecrate you as my talisman.

Making someone think about you

If you want to make someone think about you, and in this way help a relationship develop slowly but surely, use this spell. Remember that this kind of relationship, which begins with a thought and develops slowly into a healthy relationship, is the genuine thing our soul is seeking.

This is what you have to do:

1. Choose a night when there is a full moon and go outside, holding a coin in your hands.

2. Put the coin in a box and bury it.

3. Take some seeds from a rose and use them to write the name of the person whom you want to get to think about you on the ground.

4. Water the seeds every day, and as they grow, be aware that a love relationship with the person of your choice is in the offing.

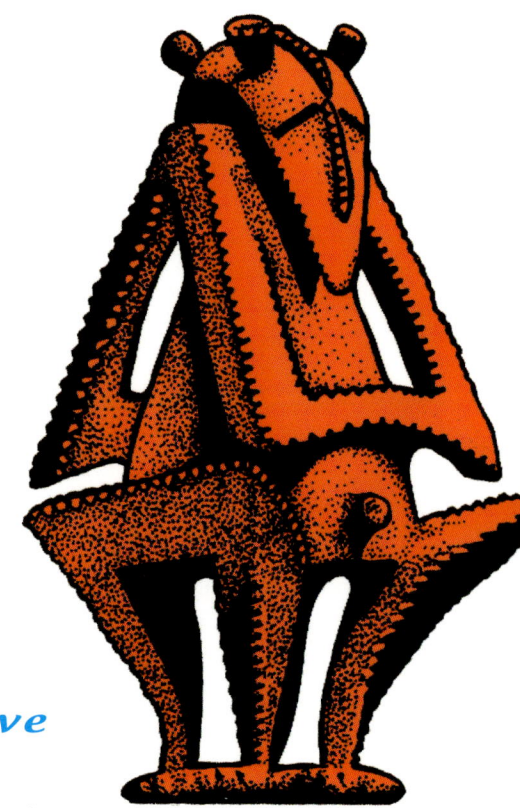

spells

The tree of love

If you want to create love energy in your life with your children, spouse or partner, this spell will help you.

This is what you have to do:

1. Take two large leaves. Draw a picture of yourself on one of them, and a picture of the specific person for whom you are doing the spell on the other.

2. Take a green thread and tie the two leaves together.

3. Look for a tree that you like, hide your leaves inside it and say:

"I call on all the elements of nature – water, air, fire and earth – to fill my relationship with goodness and love."

4. Take two coins, and bury them at the base of the tree.

spells

Releasing the woman inside you

This spell is for women only. A lot of women have a problem releasing their feminine side and taking advantage of it. If you want to release your feminine side and your feminine powers, this spell will help you.

This is what you have to do:

1. Choose a night when there is a full moon.

2. Light incense and play soft music.

3. Put on a caftan and a mask. (These represent women's mysterious side.)

4. Hold a staff in one hand and a sword in the other.

5. Stand in the middle of the room where you are performing the ritual.

6. Tap the staff on the floor eight times and say:

"I call on the goddesses of love, beauty and sexuality to help me release the woman that is locked inside me. I take my feminine powers and make them stronger."

7. Repeat these words four times, each time in a different direction – north, south, east or west – and when you face the last direction, say aloud: "I request that my feminine powers come to me."

Expressing gratitude

Giving thanks when things are going your way allows the universe to register that you would like it to continue in this manner! Taking time to perform this ritual will ground you in the joy of what you are grateful for, and assure that your thoughts remain focused on what you appreciate in life.

Timing – Monday, full or waxing moon is preferred. However, this ritual can be performed at any time and still be effective.

Candles – One straight or tapered candle in your astrological color; four small straight or votive candles – one silver, one gold, one pink, and one purple

Incense – Sage

Crystals – Clear quartz, rose quartz, and amethyst

Oil – Magnolia

Spell

For this ritual, use a spell you have written yourself, which simply states your thanks for whatever it is you are grateful for, or a general thanksgiving for the abundance of blessings in your life. Keep it simple, and hold the things, people, and feelings you are grateful for in your conscious thought as you recite your spell. End with "May my life continue to flow thus, in keeping with my highest good."

Ritual – Light the altar candle and the incense. Anoint the astrological candle working from wick to end, and carve your name into the top portion of the candle. Place it in the center of the altar, and place the crystals near its base. Anoint the small candles, from wick to end, and place them in a row in front of the astrological candle. Light the candles. Chant the spell several times, while gazing into the flame of the astrological candle, and then into the flame of each candle in turn. Allow the candles to burn down completely.

spells

The moon as a mirror of yourself

Sometimes we do things but we are not sure whether we did the right thing. Sometimes, someone is hurt by us and we don't know why. If you want to look into yourself and judge your actions, this spell will help you. This ritual is very spiritual and powerful.

This is what you have to do:

1. Choose a night when there is a full moon.

2. Meditate for one hour.

3. Stand in the center of the room and draw a circle around you.

4. Face the east and say aloud: "I am standing in the circle, I am powerful and protected now."

5. Stand with your feet together and with your arms outstretched, and say:

"I call on the power of the universe and the power of the moon to help me look into myself so that I can learn about my actions."

6. Take half a teaspoon of salt, put it on your tongue and say:

"I am loved by the power of the universe; I permit it be the judge of my actions now and forever."

7. Take a bell, and, facing north, ring it four times, saying: "I am a child of this universe. May the power of the goddess point me in the right direction and toward the correct actions for me."

8. Stand in silence to receive the blessing.

9. Wait until you feel energy surrounding you.

Candle magic for purification and protection

Protection from abuse (when you are the victim)

Timing – Tuesday, new or waning moon

Candles – Tall straight or taper candles, one each in black, white, and purple, and indigo

Incense – Patchouli

Crystals – Black obsidian, smoky quartz, and red jasper

Oil – Frankincense

Spell

When (abuser's name) approaches, my spirit expands.
My aura shines brightly, and repels all violence.
Peace reigns in my environs, now and always.

Ritual – Light two altar candles and place them in the back corners of the altar. Light the incense. Anoint the black candle, working from the wick to the end. Carve the abuser's name into the black candle and place it on the right side of the altar. Anoint the white and purple candles from end to wick, and carve your own name into the white candle. Place the white candle on the left side of the altar and the purple and indigo candles beside it, leaving as large a distance as possible between the black candle and the others. Place the red jasper near the white candle, and the black obsidian near the black candle. Place the smoky quartz near the purple candle. Light the purple candle, then the white, indigo and black candles. Chant the spell several times, and allow the candles to burn down completely.

Protection from enemies

Timing – Waning moon, beginning on a Tuesday at least seven days before the new moon.

Candles – Seven candles in each of the following colors: purple, indigo, and magenta

Incense – Pine

Crystal – Aquamarine

Oil – Pine

Spell

Stop – stop and retreat
Change thy mind forever
Stop – stop and retreat
May our lives be separate and contained
May we cease to bring one another pain
Stop – stop and retreat
Bound, you will not aggress against me again.

Ritual – Light the altar candle and incense. Carve the name of the enemy into the each of the purple candles. Anoint one candle of each color, working from wick to end. Place the anointed purple candle in the center of the altar with the anointed magenta candle on its right and the anointed indigo candle on its left. Light the purple candle, then the indigo and magenta candles. Chant the spell several times while looking into the flame of the purple candle. Visualize your enemy retreating and becoming smaller and smaller. Continue the visualization until your enemy "disappears." Allow the candles to burn out completely. Repeat the ritual each day at the same time, for a period of seven days.

Protection from gossip or slander

Timing – Tuesday, waning moon

Candles – One black and white double action candle, with black on the bottom; one indigo straight or votive candle, and one black votive

Incense – Sandalwood or citronella

Crystals – Hematite and beryl

Oil – Lilac

Other – Small nail or metal pin

Spell

Words for ill shall not be spoke,
Words for good shall pour like smoke,
Only purely shall you speak,
Lies and slander no more shall be.

Ritual – Light the altar candle and the incense. Anoint the double-action candle, working from the wick to the end. Stick the nail into the double-action candle where the black wax meets the white. Place the double-action candle in the center of your altar. Anoint the black votive candle from the end to the wick, and anoint the indigo candle from the wick to the end. Place the black candle to the left of the double-action candle and the indigo to the right. Place the stone at the base of the double-action candle. Light the candles and chant the spell several times. Allow the indigo and black candles to burn completely down. Allow the double-action candle to burn until it releases the nail. Then snuff it out and dispose of the remaining wax.

Purifying a home (space clearing)

Timing – Saturday, new or waning moon

Candles – One purple seven-knob or seven-day candle. Seven black, seven royal blue, and seven magenta straight or votive candles. Small white tea lights – on seven for each room in the home.

Incense – Myrrh or frankincense

Crystals – Bloodstone or clear quartz crystal

Herb - Basil

Oil – Yarrow or rose

Other – Flowers, holy water. (Holy water can be made by charging pure spring water with your intentions. Place your outstretched fingers over a bowl of water, and consciously charge the water with your desires and energy. When you feel the water flowing energy back to your fingers, the water is ready.)

Ritual – Light the altar candles and the incense. Place flowers in each room, and light a tea light next to each of the flower arrangements. Walk about the house with the incense, allowing it to infuse each room in turn. As you tour the house in this manner, keep thoughts of light and love flowing into the space, and banishing any negative or outside energies.

Returning to the altar, anoint the seven-knob candle, working from wick to end, and place it in the center of the altar. Anoint one black candle, working from the end to the wick. Anoint one royal blue and one magenta candle, working from wick to end. Place the black candle behind the seven-knob candle, and the magenta and royal blue candle on either side. Place the crystals near the base of the seven-knob candle. Light the seven-knob candle, then the other candles. Chant the spell. Carry the bowl of holy water to each room of the house in turn. In each room, gaze at the flame of the tea light, and chant the spell. Taking one of the flowers, dip its head into the holy water and sprinkle a small amount into the room. Allow the tea lights to burn down completely. Allow the seven-knob candle to burn just to the end of the first knob. The magenta and royal blue candles should burn down completely.

Repeat the ritual the next six nights, burning one knob of the seven-knob candle each night and using fresh magenta, black, and royal blue candles. Leave the flowers in the rooms of the home and light fresh tea lights each night as well.

Spell

I fill this space with my loving energy. My home is empty of all predecessor energy, and ready for me to fill it with my presence and experiences. Light and love are welcome – dark spirits are banished.
I proclaim this space pure and cleansed.

spells

Binding love to your life

If you want to bind real love to your life – a real love that will bring good energies and beneficent power – this spell will help you.

This is what you have to do:

1. Take three threads – pink, red and blue – and knot them together tightly.

2. While you are knotting them, imagine the person you want to be with. When you do that, think of specific character traits you want this person to have.

3. After that, tie seven more knots.

4. Put the knotted threads into the purse you use regularly until a true love enters your life. (This will happen soon.)

When you have found love, bury the knotted threads in the ground, or throw them into the sea.

spells

Going back in time

Since the dawn of history, people have wanted to remain young and beautiful and delay the onset of old age as much as possible. Although nothing can be done to prevent aging, this potion will help you remain as young as possible.

This potion is from the 14th century, and the queen of Hungary used it very successfully.

This is what you have to do:

1. Mix six drops of rosemary oil with half a glass of sunflower oil.

2. Pour the mixture onto your head and massage it slowly.

3. Close your eyes and inhale the smell into your body. Imagine it flowing into every organ of your body.

4. Take a sheet of paper and write your name on it in pink ink.

5. Put the sheet of paper in a glass you have prepared beforehand and say:

"I call on the power of the universe to enhance my charms, make me look as young as I can, and make other people see this change."

6. Take the paper out of the glass and throw it away.

7. Wash the oil out of your hair.

Soon you will look and feel different.

spells

Candle magic for termination or release

Release from negative behaviors or beliefs

Timing – Tuesday or Saturday, new or waning moon
Candles – One black, one brown, and one white taper or votive
Incense – Cedar
Crystals – Hematite and smoky quartz
Oil – Pine
Other – Small photo of yourself in an envelope

Spell

I sense what is wrong
I know what is right
I turn from the wrong
I face toward the light

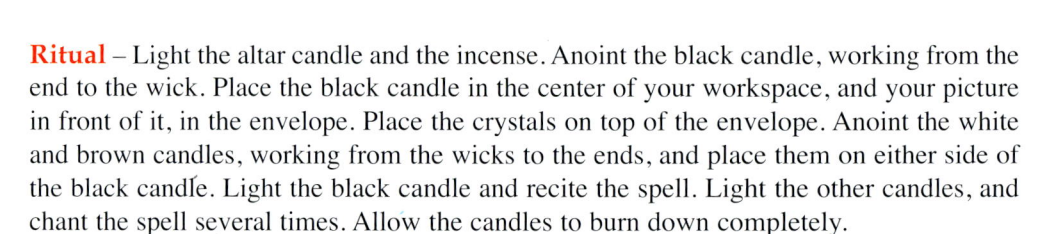

Ritual – Light the altar candle and the incense. Anoint the black candle, working from the end to the wick. Place the black candle in the center of your workspace, and your picture in front of it, in the envelope. Place the crystals on top of the envelope. Anoint the white and brown candles, working from the wicks to the ends, and place them on either side of the black candle. Light the black candle and recite the spell. Light the other candles, and chant the spell several times. Allow the candles to burn down completely.

The sun spell

We all have bad days when we feel that nothing is working for us and whatever we do is wrong. On those days, we're lacking good energies and we have to strengthen ourselves with the power of the sun, the largest source of energy in nature.

This is what you have to do:

1. Take a few items of clothing that belong to you and put them on the floor.

2. Take a few drops of St. John's wort oil and drip it in a circle around your clothes.

3. Place four yellow candles around the circle and light them.

4. Sit in the center of the circle.

5. Hold a yellow flower in each hand.

6. Gaze at the candle in front of you, concentrate and say:

"I call on the power of the sun, the power of the light, to release the spirits of darkness from me."

7. Imagine the light around you getting into your body and filling it with good light. (Try to do it for half an hour.)

8. When you have completed this ceremony, return the flowers back to Mother Earth.

Upon completion of this spell, you will feel full of good energies and nothing will be able to hurt you. Every time you feel a lack of energy, you can perform this spell.

spells

Uniting body, mind and spirit

Our body is made up of three important things: body, mind and spirit. If one of the things is not working correctly, all the other parts are affected.

Our body often wants to do something, but our mind prevents it from doing it, and vice versa. If you are in that kind of situation, or you want to prevent it from occurring, this spell can help you unite all three parts and achieve balance.

This is what you have to do:

1. Find an outdoor place where you can be alone. Take a feather, a pink ribbon and black, red, yellow and white beans with you.

2. Imagine you are opening a door outside your regular life.

3. Walk in the place you chose, stop where you feel most comfortable, and put the feather you brought with you on the ground there.

4. Take the pink ribbon and put it around the feather.

5. Place the colored beans next to the feather.

6. Pick up the feather and sit in the place where it had been lying.

7. Take a deep breath and look around you. Try to meditate in that manner for one hour while you feel nature alive around you.

When you go back home, you will feel balanced. You will feel as if your body, mind and spirit are thinking and wanting the same things. Be sure to perform this ritual once in a while.

Release from an unwanted suitor

It sometimes happens that we are desired and pursued by a person in whom we have no interest. This unwanted pursuit can become irritating and sometimes even dangerous. If you have tried to turn the person down gently, to no avail, this ritual will help you remove the person – or at least his or her unwanted attentions – from your life.

Timing – Tuesday, new or waning moon

Candles – Two white or red figure candles, one representing your own gender and one representing the gender of the unwanted suitor. The figure candles should both be of the same color.

Incense – Rue or clove

Crystals – Agate, malachite, and smoky quartz

Oil – Juniper or patchouli

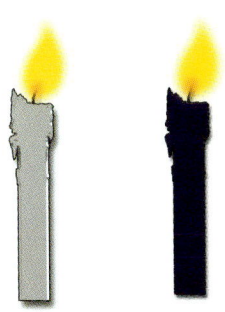

Spell
Turn around, go from me
Feel you can, feel that you are free
Turn around, let me go
No more your attention shall I know

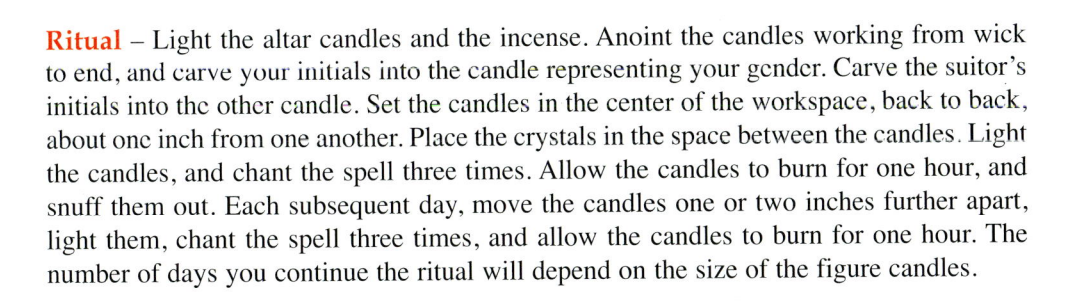

Ritual – Light the altar candles and the incense. Anoint the candles working from wick to end, and carve your initials into the candle representing your gender. Carve the suitor's initials into the other candle. Set the candles in the center of the workspace, back to back, about one inch from one another. Place the crystals in the space between the candles. Light the candles, and chant the spell three times. Allow the candles to burn for one hour, and snuff them out. Each subsequent day, move the candles one or two inches further apart, light them, chant the spell three times, and allow the candles to burn for one hour. The number of days you continue the ritual will depend on the size of the figure candles.

Spell for starting the year

In order to starting the new solar year, you have to perform this spell in the middle of the hottest season. This time of the year is the door to the new year. It is the time of maximum light and minimum darkness, and that is why it is best to call on the power of light to start your year with its full energies.

This is what you have to do:

1. Choose the room in your house that has the most windows, so you can see the sunlight from it.

2. Take two mirrors and two vases of yellow flowers. Place one of the mirrors behind the vase on one side of the room and the other mirror behind the other vase on the other side of the room, so they are opposite each other.

3. Take two yellow candles and use a pen to mark them off into six parts. Place them near the mirrors and light them.

4. When the candles burn down to the first mark, take a yellow ribbon and wrap it around one of your fingers.

5. Stand between the two mirrors and feel the light flowing all over your body. Slowly turn three times in a clockwise direction, feeling the sun's rays entering your body.

6. When you are through, stand where you are and say:

"I call on the powers of the sun to open a door to the new year for me, a door of health, prosperity, good spirits and good energies."

If you can, perform this spell for six days.

Release from a hex, curse, or "evil eye"

Timing – Saturday, new or waning moon

Candles – One black seven-knob candle and seven votives in each of the following colors: royal blue, silver or gray, magenta, and purple

Incense – Cedar

Crystals – Black onyx, black obsidian, sardonyx, and clear quartz crystal

Oil – Patchouli

Other – Photo of yourself or the person under the influence of the curse

Spell

I call upon all the forces of good, all of my guides, my angels, and my own higher powers, to converge upon this negative energy and return it to whence it originates. Send it away from me with a powerful reversal and release. May I be purified and free, and protected from its evil for all my days. I immerse myself in white light and facilitate this release.

Ritual – Light two altar candles, and place the incense between the altar candles and light it. Anoint the black seven-knob candle, from the end to the wick. Place the photo and the black candle in the center of the altar and light the black candle. Place the crystals near the base of the candle, or on the photo. Anoint one of each of the other colored candles, working from the wicks to the ends, and place them in front of the black candle, in a row from left to right. Light the candles. Chant the spell. Replace "I" with the name of the hexed person if you are performing this ritual for someone else. Allow the colored candles to burn down completely, and snuff out the black candle after one knob has burned. Repeat the ritual for the next six days, preferably at the stroke of midnight.

To increase your passion

Since time immemorial, people have being trying to find a potion that will increase their passion with their love partner. Today, the only potion that comes close to doing that is alcohol, which is a stimulant. However, the original natural formula was invented by witches. This spell will help you increase your passion with your partner (especially recommended for use during your honeymoon!).

This is what you have to do:

1. Choose a night when there is a full moon.

2. Go outside, holding a silver coin in your hand.

3. Look at the moon, and meditate by thinking of your love and imagining him/her.

4. Take four basil leaves and roll the silver coin all over them.

5. Take two glasses of red wine, put the coin in one of them and leave it for one hour.

6. Remove the coin and let your lover drink from that glass.

Soon you'll feel the passion flowing into your body.

Communication with the spiritual realm

It is a good idea to meditate for a while before beginning this ritual.

Timing – Monday, full or waxing moon

Candles – Tall taper candles – one white, one purple

Incense – Lotus

Crystals – Amethyst, celestite, and apophyllite

Oil – Myrrh

Spell

I rise upward in consciousness to meet whomever may choose to communicate with me. I exist beyond my physical sense, ready to know whatever message is there for me. I am open. I am ready. May I know the spirit realm, and may it blend with my consciousness.

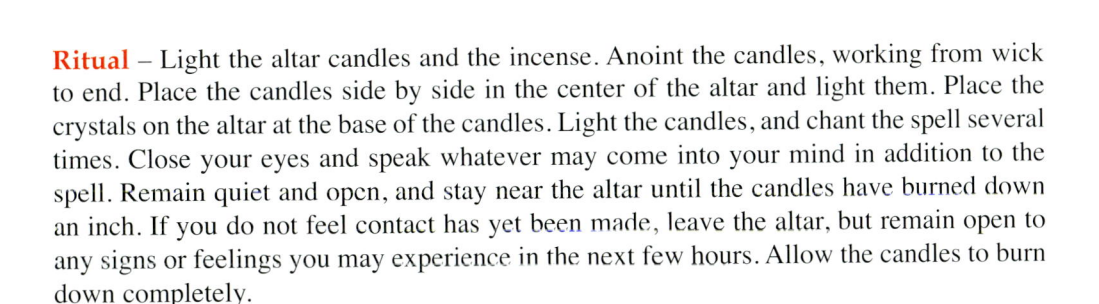

Ritual – Light the altar candles and the incense. Anoint the candles, working from wick to end. Place the candles side by side in the center of the altar and light them. Place the crystals on the altar at the base of the candles. Light the candles, and chant the spell several times. Close your eyes and speak whatever may come into your mind in addition to the spell. Remain quiet and open, and stay near the altar until the candles have burned down an inch. If you do not feel contact has yet been made, leave the altar, but remain open to any signs or feelings you may experience in the next few hours. Allow the candles to burn down completely.

A spell for reducing stress

We all suffer from stress from time to time, which debilitates our body over the long term. That is why we have to avoid stressful situations and try to reduce our exposure to them. This spell will help you reduce stress in your life.

This is what you have to do:

1. Make a small bag. It is very important that you do this yourself.

2. Take a brown pencil and write your initials on the bag.

3. Collect five dry leaves and five dry flowers and put them inside the bag.

4. Close the bag with a string and put it in a dark place in your room.

5. When you feel stress entering your life, take the bag out and put your hands inside it, feeling the power of Mother Earth. Let Mother Earth do the work for you while you visualize all your problems leaving you.

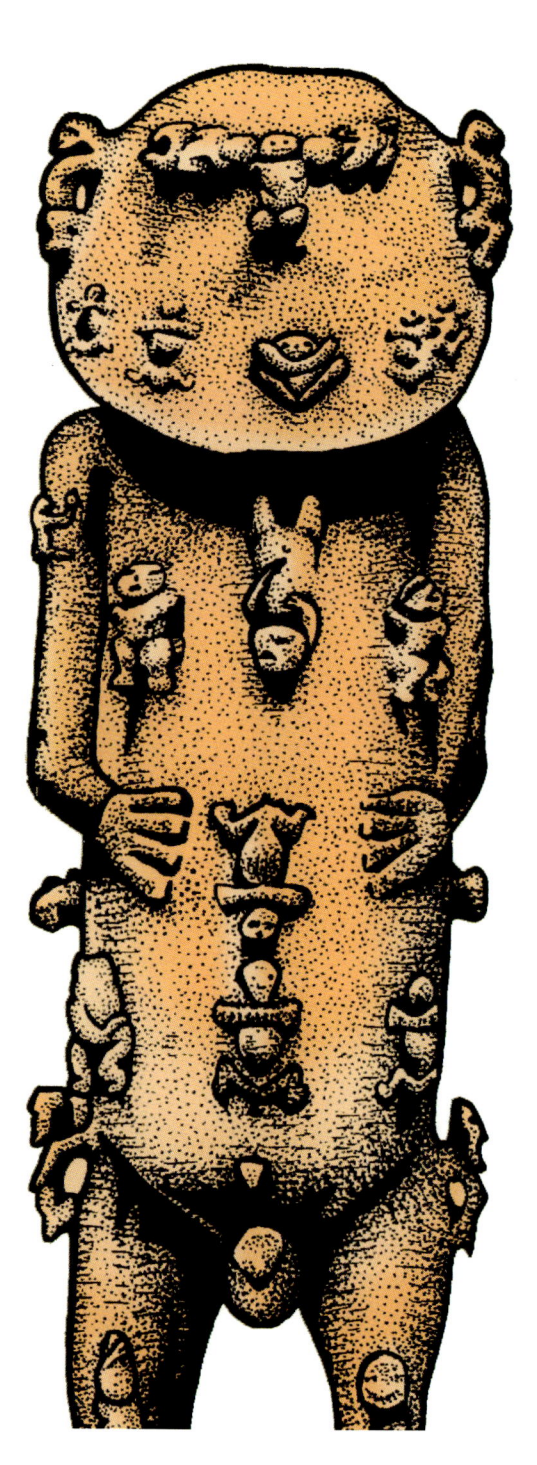

spells

Good luck charm

This charm will help you improve your fortune in life. According to the ancient Kabbala, the day you were born is your destiny, and the first letter of your name is your fortune. Since there are better and worse days on which to be born, these two things have an effect on your life.

This spell will help you usher good fortune into your life.

This is what you have to do:

1. One Sunday morning, take a gold coin.

2. Hold it in both hands and stand facing the sun in order to charge it with the sun's rays.

3. When you feel that the coin is sufficiently charged, say:

"I ask the power of the universe and the power of the sun to bring good fortune in love and in money into my life."

4. Take an old pair of shoes belonging to you and put the coin in the left one.

5. Put both shoes on, and walk in a circle four times.

6. When you are through, put the shoes next to each other in a place where no one can touch them.

7. Perform that ritual for three days.

8. On the third day, put the coin in your everyday shoes and try to wear those shoes as often as you can.

Soon you will feel good fortune entering your life.

Chamomile spell

Chamomile is a very important herb that is used in various spells. It is called the flower of equilibrium and was used to keep children from fighting all the time. This spell will help you calm your children down and give you some peace and quiet.

This is what you have to do:

1. Gather your children around you and try to make this potion together.

2. Take 40gr. of dried chamomile flowers.

3. Pour boiling water into a teapot, add the chamomile leaves to it and wait for 10 minutes.

4. Pour the potion into a bowl and leave it to cool.

5. Bring a pot containing soil inside, and let the each child plant a chamomile plant in it.

6. While they are doing that, let them say:

"Show us the charm of nature, the charm of the flowers, and tell us the spell of peace."

7. Let them wash their hands in the warm chamomile potion and tell them that they may ask the power of nature to grant them a wish.

Improving your relationship

There are times when we feel that the world is against us for no real reason. We can't get along in our marriage, and we can't get along with our children and friends, and the situation becomes unbearable. If for some reason you feel that your relationship with the people around you is strained, this spell will help you improve it.

This is what you have to do:

1. Choose a night when there is a full moon.

2. Prepare a few items that represent the elements of nature: an incense stick, some colorful flowers, a yellow candle and a bowl of rose water.

3. Put those four elements on the four sides of the room you choose, and light the candle and the incense.

4. Stand in the center of the room and repeat a few times:

"I call on the power of the four elements in nature – air, earth, fire and water – to come here and restore my balance with the people I love."

5. Invite all the people with whom you want to mend your relationship.

When the people arrive at your home, the energies you have created will already create a different atmosphere.

spells

Egyptian spell

The Egyptians believed in the power of the word. You have to be careful of what you are thinking because words create all things, for good and for evil. Sometimes even your thoughts can affect your life, because thoughts are the beginning of words, and words are the beginning of actions.

This spell will help you improve your ability to think positively. You can perform this spell on your own, with a group of friends or with your family.

This is what you have to do:

1. First, each person should cleanse himself by taking a bath with five drops of rosemary oil and a spoonful of salt.

2. Take a few sage leaves and green olives and place them in every corner of the room.

3. Take a bowl of spring water and sprinkle a little in every room in your house.

4. Everybody should stand around the bowl of spring water, holding hands, and say: "Everything that enters this place will enter with good energies; bad and evil spirits will be stopped by the herbs I put in the corners of my house."

Try to do this spell once in a while.

Harmony spell

Today, between the rat-race of life and advancing technology, we don't even have the time to stop for a little while and think of what are we doing; we just do the things we are supposed to do. This ritual will help you stop and create a harmonious environment. You can perform this spell wherever you go in the world in order to create harmony.

This is what you have to do:

1. Find a room where you can have some privacy.

2. Light an incense stick and put it in the south of the room. Light a candle and put it the east. Take two flowers and put them in the north, and take a bowl of water and put it in the west of the room.

3. Lie down in the center of the room and close your eyes.

4. Imagine that you are opening a door on to a vista of green mountains. The sun is shining everywhere. You move towards the light and warmth.

5. Slowly open your eyes and thank nature for this excursion and for creation.

6. When you have returned from the journey, write about your experience, and let it flow inside you.

The key of life

There is an old tradition of carrying an amulet when you travel or when you have an important thing to do and you need all the luck you can get. The Egyptian ankh is a good example of that, since it is a symbol of immortality and the power of protection that contains both male and female elements.

This spell will help you make your own amulet to carry wherever you go.

This is what you have to do:

1. Take two nut twigs and tie them in a shape of a small key with a brown ribbon.

2. Take the amulet, place it in the center of your forehead on a night when there is a full moon, and charge it for a few minutes.

3. Take a small bag or packet and place the amulet inside it.

4. When you have done that, you should carry this amulet on your person wherever you go, but you can also put it in your bag or in your purse.

This amulet will make you feel safe wherever you go.

Making a fresh start in life

Most of us find it difficult to make a new start in our lives – whether it is a new job or a new relationship. This spell will help you make the change as easily as possible.

This is what you have to do:

1. On a night when there is a new moon, hold a silver coin, two shells and some vervain leaves in your hands.

2. Stand outside, opposite the moon and next to the sea, and relax your body and mind.

3. Throw one of the shells into the water, and say:

"I throw all my fears into the water and I ask for a new beginning to come easily to me."

4. Take a piece of paper, write your wish and your name on it and put it inside the other shell.

5. Wrap the shell in the vervain leaves, and bury it in the sand.

Now, you just have to wait for your wishes to come true, and after that your path to success in your new venture will come easily.

spells

The balloon of success

This magic comes from China. It is air magic, which will help you achieve success in everything you desire. In China, they used to send wishes into the air in the belief that the message would float to the goddess. This air magic is directed at personal success, fortune and happiness.

This is what you have to do:

1. Wait for a windy day.

2. Look for a hill or another high open place.

3. Take a green balloon and tie a long ribbon to it.

4. When you are on the hill, hold the end of the ribbon and think about the changes and requests you want to make by means of this ritual.

5. For each wish you make, tie a knot in the ribbon.

6. Imagine your energy flowing through the ribbon to the balloon, and from there to the open sky.

7. Run with the balloon, thinking of your wishes as you do so.

8. Stop at a place where you feel comfortable and walk in six clockwise circles.

9. When you are through, untie the knots you have made, and let go of the balloon, watching it until it disappears from view.

Soon your wishes for success will come true.

A third wheel

We often feel that our relationship is being jeopardized by a third party – possibly a friend or a parent – who for some reason does not want this relationship to succeed. This situation can affect our relationship and introduce bad energies into it.

This spell will help you neutralize that effect.

This is what you have to do:

1. Choose a night when the moon is waning.

2. Choose a place where you will not be disturbed.

3. Write the name of the interfering person on a piece of paper.

4. Peel a clove of garlic and smear it over the name on the piece of paper.

5. Take an envelope, place the paper inside it, and seal it with candle wax.

6. Hold the envelope close to your heart and say:

"I ask the power of the love goddess to help me release my partner from (the name of the person)."

Repeat this four times.

7. Burn the envelope in the flame of the candle and take the ash and bury in the ground.

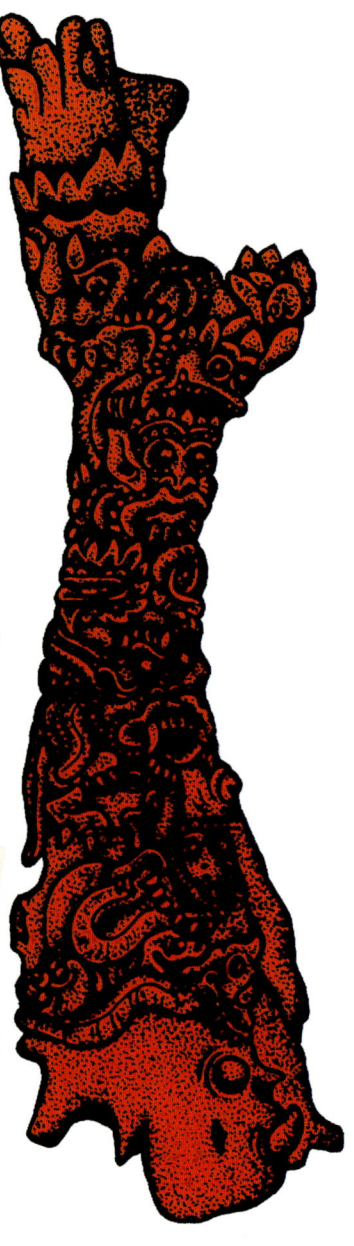

spells

To avoid divorce

If you are having problems with your marriage and thinking about getting a divorce, this spell can help you prevent it and improve your relationship with your partner, thereby reinforcing the marriage.

This is what you have to do:

1. Buy an unblemished red apple. (It would be better if you could pick an apple directly from a tree.)

2. Cut the apple in half. Make sure that you do not damage the pits.

3. Take a piece of paper and write the name of your partner on it and your own name next to it.

4. Cut out the bit of paper containing the names and place it between the two halves of the apple.

5. Imagine that the two parts of the apple are joining together and your marriage is being healed.

6. Join the two halves together with two pins.

7. When you have done that, think about your spouse, send him/her your love and ask for his/her love in return.

8. Put the apple as it is in the oven and bake it until it looks whole.

Soon you will see that your relationship is improving, and the thought of divorce will disappear completely.

Reinforcing your partner's loyalty

Many marriages end because one of the partners strays. This spell will help you to bring your partner back home where he/she belongs.

This is what you have to do:

1. Take a pair of your partner's underwear and a pair of your underwear.

2. Using a red pen, write your name on your partner's underwear and your partner's name on your underwear.

3. Tie the two pairs of underwear together with a red ribbon.

4. Put them in a red envelope.

5. Place the envelope under your pillow and sleep on it or put it in the drawer where you keep your intimate apparel.

Soon you will see a change in your partner's attitude toward you and your family.

spells

Curing depression

With its bad vibrations, depression can affect the people around you. It is like an illness. That's why you should stay away from people who make you depressed, or, if you are depressed, try to keep away from other people in order not to affect them. Things you can do include putting on cheerful music, spending time with people you like or watching a comedy. If none of this helps, try this spell.

This is what you have to do:

1. Take a few cloves of garlic and put them in a bowl.

2. Pour vinegar over the garlic until it is covered.

3. Put the bowl next to your bed and go to sleep. (The mixture might change color because of the bad energies.)

4. In the morning, take the mixture and bury it in the ground outside.

Perform that ritual for two nights, and the next day, you will feel a big difference in your mood.

spells

To conceive a baby son

Many cultures believe that bringing a son into the world is a great gift, since it ensures the continuation of the family line. This spell can help women to conceive a son.

This is what you have to do:

1. Choose the most fertile day of the month.

2. Take a red rose and put it on the table.

3. Light a red candle and a pink candle and place them next to the rose.

4. Light a yellow candle and place it in front of the two other candles to create a triangle.

5. Stand next to the table, and say out loud:

"I call on the power of the universe to bring me a new soul in the form of a son."

6. Close your eyes and imagine your son coming toward you as you smile at him and take him in your arms.

7. Take the rose and put it under your pillow for one night.

All you need now is your partner's cooperation...

To rid your body of an illness

Every time our body contracts an illness, it is something that is connected to the soul. Since body and soul are connected, they affect each other. So if you have an illness, try to see which part of your body it affects, and try to think whether you are using this part as you should. It could be your stomach, your heart, etc.

This spell will help you to alleviate your illness.

This is what you have to do:

1. Put a little salt onto a silver coin.

2. Boil some water in a pot and pour the salt from the coin into the pot.

3. Let the salty water cool off and pour a little of it onto the coin. Use the coin to wipe the water onto the hands and feet of the person who is ill.

4. Take a green candle, light it and make circles with it around the sick person. While you do that, call out his name and request that his health be restored.

5. Place the candle next to the person's bed until it burns down.

The very next day, the person will feel a lot better.

Distance healing

If you want to heal someone who is not nearby, this spell can help you.

This is what you have to do:

1. Take an onion and write the name of the person you want to heal on it.

2. Plant the onion in a pot or in your garden with four drops of rosemary oil, a shell and a feather. Cover it with a stone and spread soil over the whole thing.

3. Put a horseshoe on it.

Soon the person you wanted to heal will feel better.

Heal your cat

If your cat got into a fight and got himself injured, this spell will help you heal him. Remember that cats have spiritual powers, and they are closely linked to spirits.

This is what you have to do:

1. Light a green candle.

2. Put your cat on your lap and soothe it gently until it is relaxed and comfortable.

3. Close your eyes and call on the spirits of the universal vet to endow your hand with healing powers.

4. After a few minutes, you will feel your hands getting warm and moving to specific places on your cat's body.

5. Close your eyes, let your hands lead, and imagine the colors of the rainbow flowing from your hands into the cat.

6. When you feel your hands stop moving, thank the spirit that helped you.

spells

Bringing a missing pet back home

If your dog, cat or other pet has gone missing, use this spell to bring it back home.

This is what you have to do:

1. Put some food in the pet's bowl.

2. Light a white candle next to it and say out loud:

"I call on the power of the universe to protect my pet and to help me bring it back home today."

3. Leave the candle until it burns down.

In a few hours or a few days, your pet will return home.

Prosperity spell

Throughout history, not only in modern times, people have been attracted to money and prosperity. Money has always given a sense of power. If you want to attract money and prosperity into your life, this spell will help you.

This is what you have to do:

1. Take four green candles and ten coins.

2. Wash the coins in salt water.

3. Take four plates and arrange them in a circle.

4. Place one coin in the center of each plate.

5. Place one candle on top of each coin and light it.

6. Put the other six coins in the center of the circle you have made.

7. Say out loud:

"I call on the power of the universe and the power of prosperity to bring money into my life."

8. Concentrate on the candlelight and think of what you will do with the money.

9. Let the candles burn down.

10. If your need is genuine and your request is really necessary for you at this time, you might feel a windfall coming into the room. If it does, thank the powers of the universe for helping you.

You can perform this spell once in a while.

spells

Winning the lottery

Each of us daydreams at least once in our life about what would happen if we won the lottery. This spell will help you win the amount you need in order to live your life properly.

This is what you have to do:

First, you have to fill out a lottery ticket:

1. Light one green candle for each of the numbers in order to fill the ticket during the spell.

2. Sit in front of the candles and watch each one, trying to see a number in its flames.

3. Fill out the lottery ticket according the number you saw in each candle.

4. Snuff out the candles and leave them as they are for three days while you send the ticket.

The wishing stone

Every one of us has secret wishes. This spell employs a special stone to help make your wishes come true.

This is what you have to do:

1. Choose a stone you like. It can be a stone you found outdoors or it can be your birth stone.

2. Make a hole in the center of the stone.

3. Wash the stone well with running water.

4. Take a pen and write your wish on it. Make sure that your wish is very clear.

5. Wait for the sunset and cover your wishing stone with soil.

6. Take a red ribbon, tie a knot in it and put it next to the stone.

7. Take some flour and mix it with water.

8. Place the mixture inside the hole in the stone.

9. Stand opposite the sunset, holding the stone in your hands, and say your wish out loud.

10. Bury the stone in the ground and imagine that your wish is coming true.

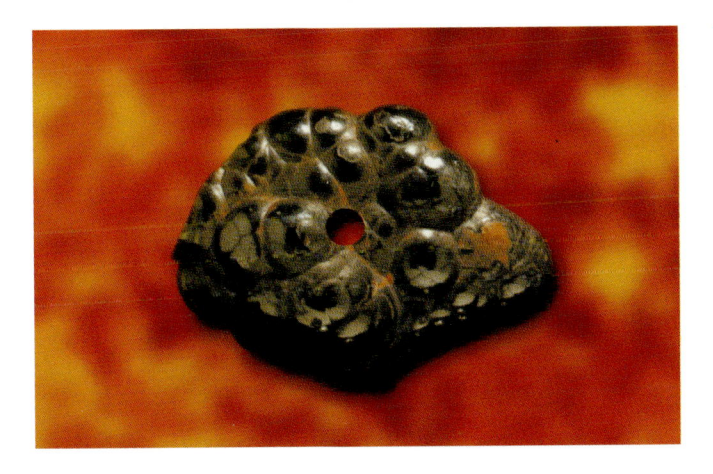

The horseshoe spell

In many cultures, a horseshoe is a symbol of good luck, especially if there are nails in it. This is because each nail symbolizes a year of good luck. This spell will help your wishes come true quickly.

This is what you have to do:

1. Get a horseshoe.

2. Use a brush to clean the horseshoe so that you can see through every hole.

3. Light a green candle in a dark room and sit in front of it.

4. Take seven small pieces of paper and write one wish on each of them. (Make sure that your wishes are very clear.)

5. Roll up the pieces of paper and insert them into the holes of the horseshoe. Make sure to do so from left to right.

6. Extinguish the candle.

7. Put the horseshoe wishes in a box and hide it in your room.

8. After six months have elapsed, open the wishes and see which of them have come true. Remove the wishes that have come true from the horseshoe.

You will be surprised how many of your wishes have come true.

The key to a successful life

The Gypsies believed that finding a key is a sign of a good luck in work, love, money, etc. This spell will help you bring all these good things into your life with the help of a key.

This is what you have to do:

1. Light a green candle in your room.

2. Take a key you no longer use and hold it in your hand.

3. Imagine that you are standing in front of a door leading to your wish, and that you are reaching out and opening it.

4. Take a piece of paper and a green pen, draw the door that you imagined before and write your wish on the door.

5. Cover the key with the candle wax and bind it together with the paper.

6. After the wax cools, blow out the candle.

7. Make a small fire outside and burn the key with the paper. As you do that, make your wish again, and imagine the door opening and you walking through it.

8. Have faith in your wish and in the power of the universe to grant it soon.

spells

The mother-in-law spell

A lot of marriages suffer from the mother-in-law's attitude toward the bride or groom. Every relationship is ultimately affected by this attitude or by having to bend to the mother-in-law's will. This spell will help you win your mother-in-law's love – by sending your love to her!

This is what you have to do:

1. Choose a Friday night when there is a full moon for this spell.

2. Take a sheet of white paper and write your wish on it. Remember that your wish has to come right from your heart.

3. Light a blue candle and place it next to the sheet of paper.

4. Take a pin with a yellow head and pierce the candle in such a way that the point of the pin emerges from the other side.

5. Look at the flames of the candle and imagine the warmth of your mother-in-law flowing through you.

6. Let the candle burn down.

7. Take a rose bulb and put another pin with a yellow head in it.

8. Bury the bulb outside in the garden.

Soon you will notice how your mother-in-law's love is growing in parallel with the bulb you planted.

spells

Finding your magic word

If you want to find your magic word, the word that will make you feel stronger and fill you with faith, this spell will help you.

This is what you have to do:

1. Light a blue candle.

2. Take a dictionary and sit quietly in your room.

3. Close your eyes and turn the dictionary around seven times.

4. Turn the pages with your eyes still closed.

5. When you feel ready, stop turning the pages and leave your hand on the page you chose.

6. With your eyes still closed, move your finger up and down all over the page; when you feel sure, stop moving your finger.

7. Open your eyes and see which word is under your finger. This is your magic word.

You can use this word whenever you need to get energized or whenever you would like to change the vibrations around you.

The Justice spell

We know that there is often no connection between the law of the land and justice. If you find yourself in a situation in which you feel that the law is not being just with you, and you want to do something about it, this spell will help you.

This is what you have to do:

1. Write the word JUSTICE on a piece of paper.

2. Light a yellow candle and place the paper to its right.

3. Take another piece of paper, write your name and address on it, and place it to the left of the candle.

4. Light twelve more candles in the colors you want, and arrange them in a circle next to the first candle.

5. Stand in front of the candles and say:

"I ask for protection from the law and I request that the law uphold the justice that is due to me."

6. Let the candles burn down and wait for your wish to be fulfilled.

spells

Uniting your family

If you want to unite your family and draw all the children together so that they feel close to one another, this spell will help you.

This is what you have to do:

1. Fill a bottle with water from a river.

2. Make a fire with some small branches.

3. Take a few leaves and on each one of them, write one of the names of the people in your family whom you want to unite.

4. Boil the river water and put the leaves in it.

5. Take a red candle and inscribe the name of your family members on it.

6. Light the candle.

7. Take the same number of ribbons as the number of family members and tie them together.

8. Remove the pot from the fire and let it cool off.

9. Take the ribbons and bury them outside.

10. Take the ashes from the fire, put them on the place where you buried the ribbons and repeat several times:

"Unite, happy family."

11. Plant a rose bush on top of the place.

As the rose grows, so the bond between your family members will become stronger.

spells

Magnet potion for romance

Every one of us is looking for his other half. This journey can take our entire lives, and sometimes it never ends. Most of the time, the partner we want is not interested in us, and vice versa. If you want to attract love or romance into your life, you can make a potion called magnet oil to help you "magnetize" your desired partner's attention. This potion can also be good for an existing relationship.

This is what you have to do:

1. Mix four drops of sandalwood oil, four drops of rosemary oil and four drops of rose oil together.

2. Spread the magnet oil you have made over a red candle.

3. Light the candle for two hours every day until the candle has burned down completely.

Soon you will see a change in the person for whom you performed the spell.

If you performed this spell for an existing relationship, you will see how you and your partner achieve harmony.

To bring your lover back

If your lover has left you, or your relationship has broken up and you want to bring your lover back to you, this spell can help you. Before using it, I suggest that you sit quietly and decide whether this partner is really the one you want. Do you love him/her for the right reasons?

This is what you have to do:

1. Choose a Saturday night for this spell.

2. Take a box of pins and an onion.

3. Take one pin and insert it into the onion. As you do so, try to invest all of your passion and imagine that each pin you insert is like putting a thought into your lover's mind.

4. Continue inserting pins into the onion and say:

"I wish that all my passion and love for the one I want, ... [say the person's name], would enter his/her mind as easily as these pins enter the onion. You will think of me night and day until you say you love me."

5. When you are through, leave the onion in the sunlight to be charged.

You will have to repeat this ritual for three days. On the last day, take the onion and plant it with love and passion. Soon your lover will come back to you in a different way.

Spell for "saying without saying"

We often have a partner to whom we cannot open our hearts and say what we really feel. Sometimes feel that our partner is not making much of an effort to please us, but we are too bashful to say what's on our mind and in our heart. This spell will help you tell your partner what's on your mind without really confronting him/her.

This is what you have to do:

1. Take a photo of your partner and a crystal ball. (If you don't have a crystal ball, you can use a magnifying glass instead.)

2. Place the crystal over the image of your partner's face until the eyes and the mouth appear to move.

3. When you see that, tell the person in the photo what you feel about him/her and what you want them to do.

Try to be honest with yourself. By performing this spell, you will send your partner the message, and he/she will soon respond to the thought you sent them.

Getting rid of an unwanted lover

As we said before, it sometimes happens that precisely the partner you don't want is the one that desires a relationship with you. First, you have to decide whether this relationship is really not for you. Once you have decided that you are stuck with a lover who has not yet understood that you are not interested in his/her love, this spell will help you make your point clearly.

This is what you have to do:

1. Choose a Friday night for this spell.

2. Take a purple candle and a bell.

3. Light the candle, and ring the bell five times.

4. Take a sheet of white paper and draw a circle in the center of it; then draw a smaller circle on the left side of the paper.

5. Take an orange and squeeze some of its juice onto the paper.

6. Fold up the paper as small as you can. While doing so, imagine that you are folding up the relationship you want to terminate.

7. Burn the paper in the candle flame.

8. Dip your finger in the ashes and write on a white paper the name of the person with whom you want to end the relationship.

9. Wrap the remaining ashes in the sheet of white paper and seal it with candle wax. As you are doing so, imagine that you are sending your unwanted lover away with loving thoughts and good wishes.

10. Bury the paper with the ashes in your garden and wait for the big change to take place.

spells

To conceive a daughter

If you want to have a daughter, you have to perform this spell during the most fertile time of the month you plan to fall pregnant.

This is what you have to do:

1. Make a doll that resembles you as closely as possible, and make it look pregnant.

2. Put some hairs from your brush onto the doll's head.

3. Dress the doll in clothes that are similar to what you are wearing.

4. Put the doll on a red scarf sprinkled with lavender oil.

5. Take it to a completely dark room, light a red candle and place it to the left of the doll.

6. Take a sheet of white paper and write on it:
7. Fold the paper and place it under the doll.

"I would like to conceive a daughter."

8. Place the doll beside your pillow and imagine your wish for a daughter coming true. Imagine the birth of your daughter.

Wait for the news that you are pregnant, and then, during your first ultrasound exam, you will recognize the power of this spell.

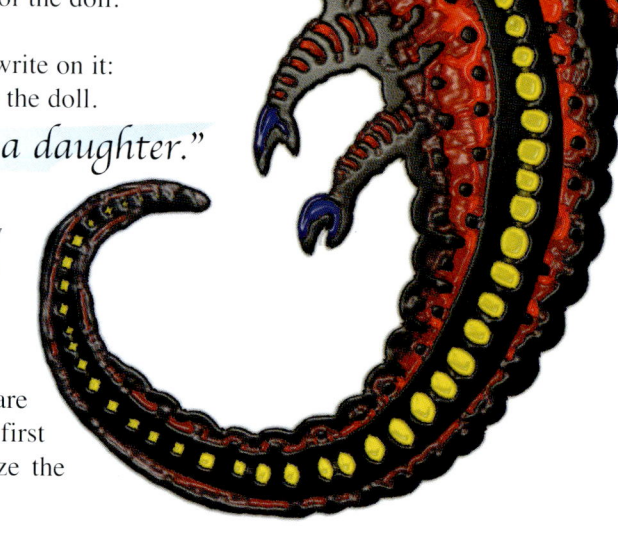

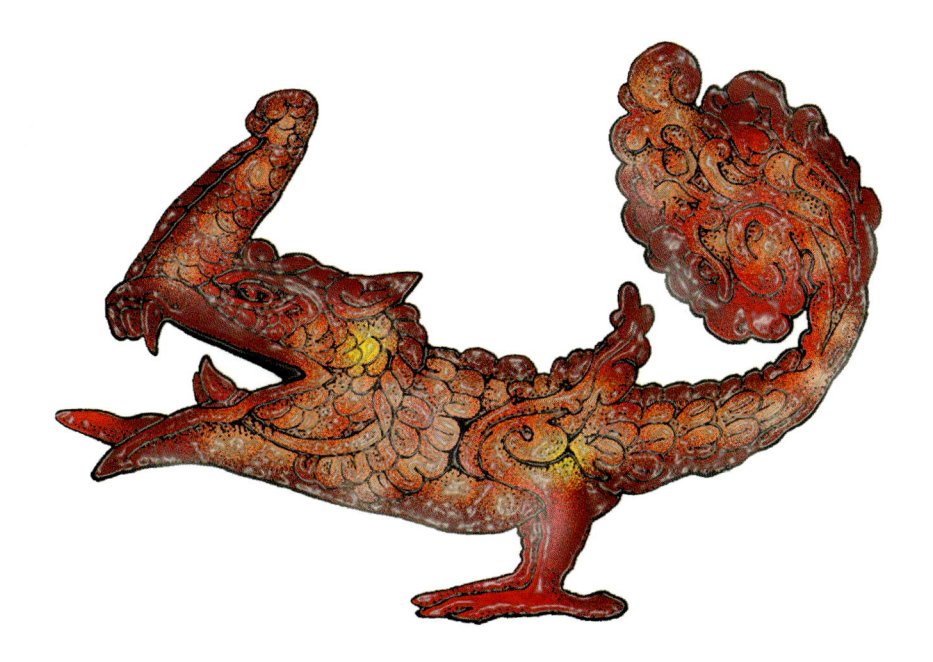

Spell for improving health

First, we have to understand that disease is a sign of the way we live our lives and the way we think about the things that happen to us. If we become ill, or someone close to us does, this spell can lead to improved health.

This is what you have to do:

1. Place a horseshoe in salt water in order to purify it.

2. When it is clean, bury it in the sick person's garden. Leave the tip sticking out of the ground, so it can be charged by the energy of the sun and the moon.

3. While you are burying it, say out loud:

"I ask the energy of the sun and the moon to charge this iron with full energy and to transfer it from here to ... [say the name of the sick person]."

Improving your eyesight

If you want to improve your eyesight, this Gypsy spell will help you. Insight and eyesight go together. If you are improving your insight by using your intuitions and feelings, your eyesight will also improve. The only reason our eyesight is damaged is because we use it more.

This is what you have to do:

1. Boil spring water with some saffron, since the saffron is also good for eye ailments.

2. Fill the bathtub with water and add the spring water with the saffron to it.

3. Sit in the bathtub and close your eyes.

4. Imagine a white light entering your eyes and flowing all over your body. Imagine that the light is clearing your eyes until all you can see is the white light.

5. Sit in the bathtub for at least an hour.

Try to do this three times a week and you will soon feel the change.

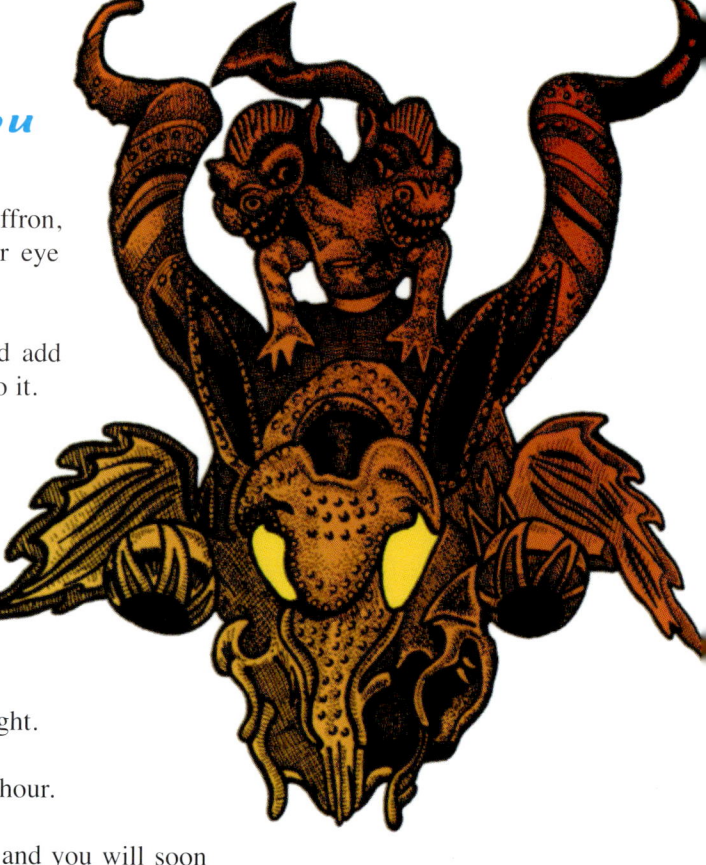

spells

To create a week of wealth

If you want to create a week of success and wealth, this spell will help you do so.

This is what you have to do:

1. Choose a Saturday night for this spell.

2. Light a yellow candle and place all the coins from your purse around it.

3. Cover the coins with a scarf and say:

"I thank the universe for the money I already have."

4. Let the candle burn down.

5. On Monday, perform the same ritual, but add the coins you have in your purse to the ones from the previous time.

6. Every day for that week, perform this ritual of lighting the candle, adding coins and giving thanks for the money you already have.

After performing the spell for a week, you will feel a change regarding the money in your life. You will feel money approaching.

LIMIT OF LIABILITY

The accuracy and completeness of the information contained in this book and the opinions stated herein are not guaranteed or warranted to produce any particular results, and the advice and techniques contained herein may not be suitable for every individual. Neither the publisher nor the author shall be liable for any loss of profit or any other damages, commercial or other, including but not limited to special, incidental, consequential, or other damages.

The information in this book is not meant to serve as a substitute for expert medical advice or treatment. It is designed to help you make informed choices. Since every individual is unique, a professional health care provider must diagnose conditions and supervise treatment for each individual health problem. If an individual is under a physician's care and receives advice that is contrary to the information provided in this book, the physician's advice should be followed, because it is based on the unique characteristics of that individual.